LOOKING FOR THE PERFECT BEAT BRINGS YOU INTO THE BOOTH WITH SOME OF THE BIGGEST SPINMASTERS

AFRIKA BAMBAATAA: His name means "affectionate leader." One of the turntable pioneers in hip-hop, the "Master of Records" led a generation into the 1980s with inspired mixes, break-dancing competitions, and experimental music.

JUAN ATKINS: Detroit's "Godfather of Techno" launched a new musical genre, and kept discriminating audiences of dancers on the floor during the late 1980s rave explosion in Britain, five thousand dancers showed up for his first gig in London.

DJ TRON: One of the biggest names in hardcore, Tron's sets—as well as his album, *Chrome Padded Cell*—are distinguished by a merciless onslaught of the hardest sounds available. He says, "I'll end a song abruptly, begin with something completely shocking, and do things throughout that nobody would expect. I want to be the David Lynch of techno."

Plus DJ Spooky, The Chemical Brothers, Liam Howlett from the Prodigy, Limp Bizkit's DJ Lethal, Coldcut, Andy Smith of Portishead, Prince Paul, Paul Oakenfold, and many more!

"We enjoy what we do, and seeing people happy!"
—Jumping Jack Frost

LOOKING FOR THE PERFECT BEAT

The Art and Culture of the DJ

Kurt B. Reighley

POCKET BOOKS

New York   London   Toronto   Sydney   Singapore

An *Original* Publication of MTV Books/POCKET BOOKS

 POCKET BOOKS, a division of Simon & Schuster, Inc.
1230 Avenue of the Americas, New York, NY 10020

 MTV Music Televison, and all related titles, logos and characters are trademarks of MTV Networks, a division of Viacom International, Inc.

Copyright © 2000 by Kurt B. Reighley

ISBN: 0-671-03869-9

First Pocket Books trade paperback printing February 2000

10 9 8 7 6 5 4 3 2 1

POCKET and colophon are registered trademarks of Simon & Schuster, Inc.

Cover design by Lisa Lucas
Front and back cover photograph: Des Willie/Redferns/Retna

Printed in the U.S.A.

Acknowledgments

First and foremost, my eternal gratitude to all the DJs who were interviewed for this book: Afrika Bambaataa; Barry Ashworth of Dub Pistols; Juan Atkins; Peter Calandra; Tom Rowlands and Ed Simons of the Chemical Brothers; Jonathan More and Matt Black of Coldcut; Steve D'Acquisto; DJ DB; DJ Lethal of Limp Bizkit; DJ Rap; DJ Skribble; DJ Soul Slinger; DJ Spooky; DJ Tron; Alec Empire of Atari Teenage Riot; Richie Hawtin aka Plastikman; Heather Heart; Liam Howlett of the Prodigy; Jumping Jack Frost; Kemistry & Storm; Robbie Leslie; David Mancuso; Kurtis Mantronik of Mantronix; Mixmaster Morris; Emily Ng aka DJ Emily; Paul Oakenfold; Peanut Butter Wolf; Prince Paul; Ben Dubuisson and Scott Hendy of Purple Penguin; Anita Sarko; Jesse Saunders; Andy Smith; Rob Swift of the X-ecutioners; and producer Bill Laswell. Extra special thanks to François K. for providing essential names and phone numbers. There were several candidates whom I approached for interviews, but fell through the cracks as deadlines loomed—most notably Danny Tenaglia, Carl Craig, Grooverider, DXT (aka Grandmixer D.ST) and Eddie "Flashin'" Fowlkes—to whom I tip my hat for their cooperation nonetheless.

For assistance in setting up interviews and tracking down research materials, I owe debts of varying degrees to the following individuals: Eric Holt; Blue at Wheels of Steel; Laura Swanson and Tommy McKay at A&M Records; Carleen Anderson at TVT Records; Dan Cohen and Alison Tarnofsky at Astralwerks; Judy Miller at Motormouthmedia; Jeff at Ninja

Tune; Stephanie Lees at Pitch PR; Jennie Boddy at Interscope; Neil Lawi at Columbia Records; Noah at Liquid Sky Music; Matteo Segade; Julie Underwood and Shelby Meade at Nasty Little Man; Michelle Ferguson, Sarah Apfel and all at MFPR; Brittany Somerset at Praxis Public Relations; Sioux Z. and all at Formula PR; Gamall Awad at Backspin; Michael Yim at Stud!o K7; Andy Shih at Oxygen Music Works; Daniel Wang; Christine Muhlke and Eric Demby at *Paper* magazine; June Joseph; Hannah Sawtell at Planet E; Asya Shein at Undaground Therapy; Craig Karpel at the Karpel Group; Hillary Siskind at Tommy Boy Records; Rita Johnson at ModCom; Tamara Palmer at *Urb* magazine; Michael Paoletta at *Billboard;* Regina Joskow-Dunton at Slash/London Records; Caroline Killoury at Fruit Management; Felice Ecker and all at Girlie Action; William Werde; Steve Cohen at Music & Art; Steve Lau at Kinetic Records; Nicole Blackman; Janet Reinstra at Luma Records; and Caron Bañez at DMC. A special shout-out to all the various and sundry editors (in addition to those already mentioned) who have assigned me pieces that served as preliminary research for this massive undertaking, including Scott Frampton at *CMJ New Music Monthly;* Joe Banks, Rob Cherry, and Dave Segal at *Alternative Press;* Darren Ressler at *Mixer;* Jackson Griffith at *Tower PULSE!;* Randy Bookasta at *Raygun;* Kathleen Wilson at *The Stranger;* and Jackie McCarthy at *Seattle Weekly.* Mea culpa to anyone I've overlooked—it doesn't mean I don't love you, only that I'm scatterbrained.

It's preposterous to suggest I could have ever written this book without the countless contributions and unbridled enthusiasm of my friend, muse, and frequent DJ partner Matthew Eugene Lemcio. I'd also like to single out Alex Calderwood and Jared Harler of ARO.space and Tasty Shows for giving me my first professional DJ gig, and Hal Angel of Cherry Bomb for keeping me on board throughout that exciting first year. Rob DiStefano of TWISTED gets a big kiss, too, for taking me out for my very first spin on the wheels of steel on that afternoon so many years ago.

For hand-holding, brainstorming and other forms of physical, emotional, and psychic massage, the following friends deserve a drink (or five) on me: Barbara Mitchell; Judy McGuire; Paul Bloch; Dan Renehan;

David Brockman; Kristy Ojala; and particularly Richard Martin, who helped me overcome an especially nasty episode of writer's block.

For their efforts behind the scenes and in the trenches, let us not forget my wonderful agent David Dunton at Harvey Klinger; the best editor a boy ever wished for, Paul Schnee, and his diligent right hand, Calaya Reid, at Pocket Books; Eduardo Braniff and Liz Brooks at MTV Books; Diana Adams for the jacket photos; and Lisa Lucas and Matthew Schaefer for their hard work on the art and design front.

For Eugene

Contents

LOOKING FOR THE PERFECT BEAT

Preface

Many years ago, in a sonic galaxy far, far away, everyone supposedly wanted to be a rock and roll singer. Today, everyone wants to be a DJ—even if they don't know it yet. Anyone who has ever had any sort of opinion on a song or flipped the radio dial in search of more pleasing tones is really just expressing his or her inner DJ.

But DJs are definitely more than breathing jukeboxes—in fact, many don't even take requests! They are architects and alchemists, sorcerers and psychologists, all rolled into one. They may take center stage as unstoppable entertainers or mysteriously provide the sound-track from a dimly lit corner, shifting the focus elsewhere. Whatever the scenario, DJs have the power and the honor to invoke the range of human emotion.

> The music selector is the soul reflector.
> —Deee-Lite's Lady Miss Kier

Today's DJ comes in every conceivable color and flavor, and their sounds are just as varied. But whether they rock the decks with hip-hop beats and tricks or keep the house music flowing seamlessly all night long, there's a certain transcendent joy that they all share. Far more than just knowing what song to play at what time, the skilled

DJ is on a mission to transform the way you hear music, just as their ears have been transformed in learning the craft.

Those who take DJing seriously consider it an art form as legitimate as any other. And as with other forms of art, there are certain bits of wisdom that a DJ may pass on to a newcomer, but after that the budding DJs are on their own to learn for themselves and make their mark. Emulating another's style may be helpful to get the ball rolling, but it's the intuition and unique design of an individual that is called into play most in creating a good DJ.

Mastering the art is both easier than you think and harder than you think. Put enough dedication and passion into it and you'll be up and running with the basics in no time. But it is also a never-ending learning curve—always up, thankfully never down—where the intricacies and finer points reveal themselves every time you practice. The most important lesson? There is absolutely no limit to your own imagination.

Finding records that work well together may be likened to finding compatible lovers. When you stumble on—excuse me, I mean *carefully execute*—a truly effective mix, the songs seem to bounce off each other perfectly in a natural union. There is a palpable energy exchange between the songs as they romance each other. Synergy. In short, it's just about the most fun you can have with your hands.

But when records do not go well together (which may be due to any number of factors, such as different tempos, keys, or even emotions), it can be like strained, awkward sex, where none of the clumsy parts mesh up properly. (DJs call such mixes train wrecks.) In those cases, as with failed love experiments, it's probably best to keep looking until a more suitable partner is found.

Become a DJ and you will discover connections between disparate pieces of work that no one might have ever guessed would have any relation to each other. Go ahead and mix that Lil' Kim song with your latest drum and bass twelve-inch single—you could be pleasantly surprised at the outcome. Give Steve Martin a rhythm to be funny to. You'll never know if Frank Sinatra sounds good backed by a lush, ambient sound environment until you try. Don't quite like how a song is arranged? Grab two copies, play composer, and make your own live remix.

No matter what you do, you are likely to widen that open-minded aural circle in your head and take your appreciation of music to a whole new level of enjoyment and understanding. If you're not already a musician, this might just be your gateway to making your own music, as it has been for many, and you'll be equipped with the knowledge of what makes a potent song structure. And, best of all, your work may soothe someone else's soul or simply give them the finest night out they've ever had, two of the most amazing compliments you could ever receive.

If you've not yet let that inner DJ out of the box, what are you waiting for? Hopefully, the lessons and voices of *Looking for the Perfect Beat* will be just what you need to light that fire under your ass. DJing—it's not just a job; it's truly an adventure.

Tamara Palmer
Co-editor, *URB* magazine
September 1999

The author at his first gig.

Introduction: Who Do You Think You Are?

DJs are artists. Their handiwork isn't complete until shared with an audience, where it takes on new meanings in the lives of those who experience it.

So it is no wonder that most artists, including DJs, are reluctant to reveal themselves before they're confident in their abilities. The globe is teeming with Emily Dickinson–esque DJs who refine their craft in seclusion. Fearing premature rejection, they practice and perfect in locked bedrooms, waiting for the ideal moment to spring forth, fully developed, captivating the world with their distinctive aesthetic and polished skills.

I was not one of them.

If I claimed I had never contemplated being a DJ, I'd be lying. I have been an avid record collector and dance music enthusiast for the better part of twenty years. My writing career has offered me opportunities to spend time chatting with some of the greatest DJs in the world.

One afternoon, many years before I ever stepped up to the decks professionally, I had beseeched my pal Rob, who, as the driving force behind one of the premier U.S. underground dance labels, knew plenty about the craft, to teach me the basics on two turntables. I spent hours under his patient gaze trying to mix two records that today I'd slap together as fast as a peanut butter sandwich. But that day, I didn't get much further than the: "Well, that wasn't a *complete* train wreck" stage.

Aside from relentlessly buying vinyl, I made no more attempts to further my dreams of DJing after that sole session. The task seemed too formidable. I mused about purchasing decks but never did; even when I worked in an office with a full DJ station for a year (minus the periods when one or more components disappeared to a rave somewhere), I never once practiced beat matching. For someone who'd interviewed— and criticized—as many different types of DJs as I had by then, I knew remarkably little about even the basic fundamentals.

None of which I disclosed the day Alex, a Seattle club owner, asked if I wanted to spin at his new venue. I ignored the simpering of my conscience ("You don't know what you're doing!") because I'd probably never get a second shot at living out my fantasy without lifting a finger. Finding the balls to say yes, knowing full well I'd probably make an ass of myself, was the hard part. I'd figure out the rest later.

Subconsciously, I'd engineered this invitation anyway. A few weeks previously, after insisting Alex's life was incomplete until he'd heard Shirley Bassey's disco version of Barry Manilow's "Copacabana," I'd made him a compilation cassette (no mixing—just good old-fashioned pauses between songs) of assorted oddities I thought he'd enjoy. Assuming I could translate this perverse programming talent into a live setting, he and his partner hired me to play music in the lounge area during their weekly drag contest.

Unaware of my existence—save as a writer who occasionally interviewed established practitioners—until shortly before the day I made my debut (April 1, 1998, appropriately), the gods of DJing were displeased with my brash display of arrogance. From high atop Mount Technics, they threw many obstacles and surprises in my path. Like scheduling a visit from my buddy Tamara Palmer, a top editor at *URB* magazine and seasoned DJ herself, to coincide with my premiere performance. Ditto for Carlo McCormick, a colleague from New York City's style bible, *Paper* magazine. By the time one of my tires blew out on an isolated stretch of highway while I was racing to the airport to pick up Tamara, mere hours before my gig, I was ready to change my name to Job.

Miraculously, we made it to the club on time and intact (and in a taxi). I had no headphones, no concept of how the mixer worked (mercifully, the sound engineer pointed out the cross-fader to me), and a crate of records obviously packed by the 1998 Multiple Personality Disorder poster child. My doom was imminent. The gods chuckled, then promptly forgot about me.

Yet at the end of my four-hour set, one that vacillated wildly from the wispy disco of Patrick Juvet ("I Love America") to gospel house by Ultra Naté ("Rejoicing") to an instructional record for learning short-hand, something amazing had happened. Nobody had thrown a drink in my face, pulled the plug on the power, or told me that I was the worst DJ in history. The only "properly" mixed (that is, beat matched) segment of the whole night had been a five-minute spell when Tamara fused Uberzone's "The Freaks" with Air's "Sexy Boy" while I watched in mute awe, but people had danced all night long.

When I was offered the gig as a regular residency, I said yes. It couldn't be any scarier than what I'd just faced.

But in fact, the year that followed was just as unrelentingly tough as that first night. Every week I learned a whit more about what I was doing, and my expectations of myself increased accordingly. Worse yet, as I became preoccupied with what I felt was my greatest professional shortcoming—an inability to match beats—I overlooked my biggest strength: an ear for distinctive music. The contents of my crate ceased to look like a schizophrenic had selected them; instead, some lobotomized automaton assumed that task. When I finally came to my senses and attempted to reintroduce a wider variety of sounds, I realized how much work still lay ahead of me.

Thus the creation of *Looking for the Perfect Beat* was inspired largely by a selfish impulse to use my professional station as a music writer to sit down with a clutch of DJs I admired or who had made significant contributions to the art form, to glean some useful wisdom from them. I felt confident that being forced to boil the aesthetic concerns of other DJs into concise prose would pressure me to examine my own motivations and ideas more closely.

Imagine my delight in discovering through my research that I was far from the first DJ to take the reins before he knew how to saddle up. I was greatly reassured to find that my original impulse—to stick to music that inspired me over all other concerns—was a guiding force for nearly everyone I interviewed. And eventually, I became resigned to the knowledge that as pleasant as these conversations were, I'd truly improve as a DJ only through application and practice. Rats.

When people ask me what kind of music I spin, I inevitably tense up. I've played drum and bass and 101 Strings in the same set and kept crowds dancing with a Jim Nabors song. My reactions to the question "What's your book about?" have been just as strong. *Looking for the Perfect Beat* isn't intended to be a comprehensive history of dance music or the *Who's Who of Great DJs* or a highly detailed how-to guide for rookie DJs. Let other authors concentrate on these individual angles. The only dynamic that seemed truly suitable to capture the essence of DJ culture was to move between a variety of topics and show how they interrelate.

Now that I have a modicum of DJ experience, I try to anticipate what my audience will be like, concentrate on what materials I'll need to communicate something unique and engaging to them, and aim to let the flow of the program reveal itself to me organically. It's really not so different from the way I write.

Thus, as with the records I play out, the participants' voices in *Looking for the Perfect Beat* have been judiciously edited and sequenced to create a diverse, one-of-a-kind experience engineered to speak to a wide but discerning range of listeners. Different opinions expressed herein will prompt wildly divergent responses in individual readers. Good. I won't deny that my biases are often evident from what I choose to discuss. Someone else might take the exact same materials and present them in a radically different fashion. But this isn't someone else's book.

Assuming the many veterans I spoke to for this project are to be trusted, a reliable DJ knows how to balance entertainment with education, underscored by his or her own individual aesthetic. I believe that definition holds true for any artist. If *Looking for the Perfect Beat* spares one neophyte DJ a little frustration, prompts a single pro to examine his or her art from a new angle, or just makes the reader think differently about how ideas—musical and otherwise—can be presented and combined, then I won't feel like such a jackass when I tell people I'm a DJ. Because at least I wasn't afraid to inflict my art on yet another new audience.

1 What Is a DJ?

What is a DJ?

A fairly simple question. Not so long ago, the answer was just as succinct. A DJ—an abbreviation for the slang term *disc jockey*—was an individual who entertained an audience by playing prerecorded music. That definition, originally ascribed to practitioners on radio, and later at social functions and watering holes, still holds true.

More than half a century later, this tiny abbreviation invites countless interpretations, and they keep multiplying exponentially. DJs are celebrities, drawing crowds of dancers in the thousands, breaking world records for attendance. DJs are musicians, virtuosos who elevate turntables far beyond mere mechanisms for playing back vinyl LPs, integral members of chart-topping bands, seasoned nightlife veterans filtering underground trends into Top 40 hits. DJs are modern-day shamans. And they're salespeople, too.

> DJs dictate what the people will listen to, dance to, and buy. We are the biggest promotion an artist can have. It's very rare for a radio station to take a record out of the box and put it on the air, unless it's an established artist. You can have a bona fide hit from a new artist, but radio won't touch it until it's already a hit in the streets. And that comes from the DJs.
>
> —DJ Skribble

But DJs also function as artists, educators, historians, and diplomats. They are constantly arranging and interpreting the multimedia stimuli that surround us. Via calculated juxtaposition of musical (and today, visual) materials, they influence social trends and provoke alternate ways of thinking, conducting business, or experiencing daily life. Their eclectic, mercurial collages embody our multitasking modern mind-set. And DJ techniques and aesthetics continue to infiltrate and shape other media: software, live performance, and even writing.

> My parents once said, "Oh, a DJ...that's somebody who plays records." But my first priority is to be a musician, who seriously puts a lot of ideas together in a creative way. That's what really defines DJing.
>
> —Alec Empire

DJs have existed on radio since after the turn of the twentieth century. On Christmas Eve 1906, pioneering electrical engineer Reginald A. Fessenden broadcast a holiday program that included a Handel recording. As the medium grew in popularity, so did the role of the DJ, as entertainer, spokesperson, and—most important—a conduit for new music. With the advent of nightclubs and discotheques, additional platforms for DJs emerged.

The historical epicenter of the DJ movement as it exists in its myriad forms today is New York City in the mid-'70s. During this era, two concurrent musical trends—rap and disco—radically redefined notions of a DJ's duties while slowly increasing DJs' cachet as artists and entertainers.

In the Bronx, rap innovators like Kool DJ Herc, Afrika Bambaataa, and Grandmaster Flash expanded the musical abilities of two turntables and a mixer. Cutting back and forth between isolated snippets of sound with lightning-fast dexterity and physically manipulating the surface of the record against the needle to generate unfamiliar bursts of noise, they transformed slabs of vinyl into fresh creations. Meanwhile, at

Manhattan discos, club jocks like Francis Grasso created inspired programs of interlocking songs and even began simultaneously layering passages from different records.

> A whole new venue for entertainment was created, with the disc jockey, the dancers, and the turntables. Instead of having a [musical] group performing, you were playing a recording. The disc jockey segued the music. And the dancing became part of the performance.
>
> —David Mancuso

Subsequent trends around the globe added new dimensions to the art of the DJ. The Chicago house movement of the '80s advanced ideas of how a DJ could interface prerecorded music and additional sound generators to yield new compositions. Detroit's techno scene fostered unexpected common ground between diverse genres (funk, New York disco, European synthesizer pop) and deliberately altered records via pronounced changes in frequency levels, pitch, and speed.

In Europe, the melting-pot style that began life as Balearic on the Spanish isle of Ibiza opened up the dance floor to include an almost unimaginable variety of genres. Imported to England a few years later, it soon folded house and techno into the mix and snowballed into the 1988 Summer of Love, an explosion of music, clubs, and outdoor parties that has made dance music and pop music synonymous in Europe ever since. From these roots, the harder-edged sounds of hardcore techno, jungle, and drum and bass later emerged.

As DJs have risen in prominence internationally, the worlds of music and entertainment have changed to co-opt their talents and accommodate their needs. New formats like the twelve-inch single allowed DJs to play longer versions of songs their crowd loved, which in turn meant wider exposure and opportunities for increased sales. Inventions like record pools and exclusive promotional pressings

MEET THE DJ

Afrika Bambaataa

Afrika Bambaataa is a humble man. His name, roughly translated, means "affectionate leader." But even this benevolent eminence might be tempted to banish from the kingdom any numbskull who doesn't recognize the extensive contributions he's made to musical history over a quarter century. His influence today transcends confining notions of old school versus new school hip-hop. As he wrote in the fanzine *Bomb*: "To myself, there is only one school, and that's the learning, evolving, and going through the different phases or cycles school of hip-hop."

Bambaataa was among the very first turntable pioneers (along with Kool DJ Herc and Grandmaster Flash) when rap emerged from the Bronx in the mid-'70s, celebrated for his dedication to musical diversity and the preservation of funk. His diverse tastes, inspired mixes, and vast music collection quickly earned him the title Master of Records. When rap began to infiltrate downtown New York City in the '80s, Bambaataa was there, rocking the crowd at the Roxy's Wheels of Steel on Friday nights.

But as leader of the Zulu Nation (founded in 1975), Bambaataa has also been the primary proponent of hip-hop as a force for social and political change. The block parties and breakdancing competitions organized by Bambaataa and his crew fostered cultural cross-pollination and offered a peaceful alternative to the violence of gang life.

As a recording artist, he leapt to international acclaim in 1982 with "Planet Rock," a groundbreaking fusion of hip-hop breaks with Kraftwerk's icy synthesizer lines; "Looking for the Perfect Beat" soon followed. Although he spawned a legacy of electro acts, with subsequent repercussions on Miami bass and Detroit techno, Bambaataa's own music continued evolving. In 1984, he was paired with both John Lydon (aka Johnny Rotten) on Time Zone's "World Destruction" and James Brown for "Unity."

Later on, Bambaataa's dedication to experimentation yielded collaborations with George Clinton, UB40, Nona Hendryx, and Boy George, and forays into house, reggae, and other genres. Most recently, he's worked with Uberzone, DJ Soul Singer, Leftfield, and Westbam and wrapped up a mix CD for DMC's *United DJs of America* series.

made music available to influential DJs early, creating alternate feed-back mechanisms for record companies to gauge commercial viability. Manufacturers of musical equipment began designing gear with the special needs of DJs in mind, prompting a wider range of turntables and mixers. Savvy club owners may even go so far as to customize sound systems or DJ booths to meet the specifications of men and women who work the wheels of steel in their venue.

> In the '60s, you had Jimi Hendrix. Now it's the '90s, and the turntable is the new instrument. The DJ is the guitar god for the new millennium.
>
> —DJ Lethal

> The market's completely shifted in Europe. There was an article in one of the major music publications recently saying that turntables are outselling guitars three to one.
>
> —Paul Oakenfold

TV commercials and print ads use images of DJs to hawk prod-ucts, from soda pop to sneakers to cigarettes. At a certain southern California university, students can study "How to DJ" for college credit. Even the stodgy National Academy of Recording Arts and Sciences finally buckled a few years ago and gave DJs the nod by introducing the Grammy Award for Best Remix. With such a variety of enticements, plus an increasing number of avenues of entry, some-times it feels like everybody wants to be a DJ.

> The mainstream is seeing what we do more and more. That's opening doors at corporations, opening up other media to DJs.
>
> —DJ Skribble

But the rise of the DJ also reflects a fundamental shift in daily life that transcends music. Considering how much information the average

MEET THE DJ

Paul Oakenfold

"I never expected to be sitting here ten years later talking about a scene that I started," admitted England's Paul Oakenfold recently. Then again, he probably never imagined being voted number one DJ of 1998 by the readers of *DJ* magazine. Or winding up in *The Guinness Book of World Records* as "Biggest DJ in the World." Or spending a year and a half touring the globe with U2.

Oakenfold acquired his first taste of dance music in the Big Apple in 1979, listening to Larry Levan at the Paradise Garage. Upon returning to London, he heartily embraced hip-hop, working as a party promoter, DJ, and A&R man. Then in 1985, while summering in Ibiza, he discovered the everything-but-the-kitchen-sink style of spinning dubbed Balearic and fell in love. But his initial attempts to import the sound flopped.

Two years later, he tried again to transfer the island vibe to London. This time, he quickly accumulated a dedicated flock of seasoned Ibiza vets. He even flew Balearic godfather Alfredo in to play and invited pivotal UK scene makers, just to further the cause. The party swelled in size rapidly, and by spring of '88, his crew launched Spectrum, one of the key clubs in the acid house explosion.

As dance music grew in popularity during the next decade, Oakenfold made contributions at every step. His remixes (most notably Massive Attack's epic "Unfinished Sympathy") navigate the narrow strait between underground credibility and mainstream appeal, whereas his productions with "Madchester" ambassadors Happy Mondays echoed Levan's experiments in studio chicanery.

These days, the former culinary student rarely has a free moment, and he certainly doesn't squander them resting on his laurels. Among other chores, he runs the Perfecto label, home to top sellers Grace and Man With No Name. Of late, Oakenfold's concentrated tremendous energy on cracking the United States, releasing his first domestic mix CD, *Tranceport*, and uplifting an ever-expanding audience of U.S. fans with his distinctive trance sets.

person is bombarded with constantly via mass media, there is more than a little bit of the DJ in all of us, filtering, processing, and fashioning this potential overload into some semblance of useful order.

> DJ culture is one of the most easily translated codes going on in music right now. You drop a needle on a certain beat and people will be able to respond, whether they're in Buenos Aires, Tel Aviv, or St. Petersburg.
>
> —DJ Spooky

The thirty-eight DJs surveyed for this book span a vast gamut. From a sage fifty-four-year-old bastion of New York underground disco to a smart-mouthed Chicago peddler of earsplitting, hyperfast hardcore techno, they all have roots in one or more of the aforementioned scenes. They are men and women, representing a variety of racial, sexual, and economic backgrounds; playing a broad spectrum of sounds; and pushing their discipline in countless new directions: internet media, visual art, criticism, software design.

> The DJ culture is very big now. You'll have the badass DJs and the politicians, the Michael Jordans of DJs. All those kinds of roles are going to happen. The image of DJ culture should always be diverse.
>
> —DJ Soul Slinger

> Music is always a metaphor for something else. It isn't just some sounds coming out of your loudspeakers. Most people in our generation involved with DJ culture are coming at it from the art world or graphic design or some sort of computer-literate vibe.
>
> —DJ Spooky

The guiding logic behind selecting a wide range of participants was twofold: first, to show the full historical and cultural scope of the

MEET THE DJ

Kate Auleta

DJ Soul Slinger

"DJing is a state of mind," Carlos Soul Slinger once told *DJ Times*. And few artists personify the DJ as an individual who constantly remixes culture better than he does. Since arriving in New York in 1989, Carlos has played numerous influential roles, as a DJ, producer, record label head, and owner of America's first rave boutique, Liquid Sky. Today he's recognized as one of the pivotal proponents of drum and bass in the United States.

The story of DJ Soul Slinger (his handle is an homage to R&B singer "Soul" Charles Wright) begins in his birthplace, São Paulo, Brazil, with his first clothing and cosmetics store. In the early '80s, he visited New York frequently, soaking up the work of such DJs as Larry Levan and David Morales, plus the exploding rap scene. In 1987, after one particularly inspirational sojourn abroad, he began teaching himself to mix. Two years later, he relocated to New York and opened Liquid Sky.

Soul Slinger started out spinning underground house and techno but by the early '90s had become captivated by the emerging sounds of UK breakbeat hardcore and jungle. The flagship release from Jungle Sky Records, his own 1994 single "Jungle Liquid Sky," was the first drum and bass record by an American producer.

The follow-up, the sublime "Abducted" b/w "Jungle Bossanova," pointed toward Carlos's diverse musical background. "It's impossible to be born in Brazil and not understand music, because you're always surrounded by drums, by rhythms, by dancing. Brazilian music is very eclectic, because the mix of cultures is very universal." That spirit is evident throughout both his debut full-length *Don't Believe* and his mix CD *Upload*.

Soul Slinger also plays with experimental jazz musicians, including Derek Bailey, Elliot Sharp, and Bill Laswell. His remix discography, featuring work for Deee-Lite, Soul Coughing, and DJ Spooky, reflects his key position in New York culture. New projects include tracks for the latest *This Is Jungle Sky* anthology and collaborations with DJ Wally and Afrika Bambaataa.

art of the DJ and second, to divine what traits and practices even seemingly disparate DJs share in common. Sometimes, being a superlative DJ hinges on the ability to make enlightened connections where none are readily apparent. Like any artistic discipline, DJing is deceptively simple to pick up, challenging to master, and constantly being altered and augmented by new generations.

A myriad of discussions address concerns both aesthetic and technical in the chapters that follow: the finer details of mixing; how to program a set and communicate with a crowd; and how DJs have changed the way we make, hear, and think about music. To varying degrees, all these concerns factor into the art of any DJ.

The most important thing all the participants of *Looking for the Perfect Beat* have in common is what motivated them to tackle their craft: a deep love for music and a desire to share it with others.

> DJing is a drug. There is no other thing where you can fail so easily. You can be rockin' a crowd and then suddenly clear the floor. And it's all down to you. That's what gives it the edge.
>
> —Ben Dubuisson (Purple Penguin)

2 Got to Be Real

> I don't think *disco* is a dirty word at all.
> —François K.

Disco. The term still sets many Americans' teeth on edge. Visions of tight, white polyester suits and spinning mirror balls appear before them and their blood pressure rises. To the vast majority who remember it, *disco* is a period in the late '70s when the airwaves were saturated with a single sound and KISS, Carly Simon, and the Muppets suddenly had more in common musically than previously imaginable. To youngsters, *disco* is merely a string of catchy novelty tunes, an entrenched canon of favorites by artists now perceived as one-hit wonders.

But disco was much more than this narrow memory etched on our collective consciousness. If anything, disco's apex as a trend—between 1976 and 1979—represented its nadir as a sound. The roots of disco existed long before *Saturday Night Fever*, and its sonic innovations and attendant lifestyle continue to exert terrific, though often unacknowledged, influence to this day.

Nightclubs that played records for dancing originated in France during World War II, when Nazi occupation prohibited live performances. After the war, certain venues retained the format; hiring a DJ was cheaper than employing an orchestra. In time, these spots were christened *discothèques*, a spin on the term for a movie house, *ciné-*

MEET THE DJ

Wave Music

François K.

A world-class DJ who doesn't own at least one piece of wax bearing a François K. (nèe Kevorkian) credit seems inconceivable. Since arriving in New York City back in 1975, François has exerted a discernible influence on the international pop and dance music worlds.

Hired to provide live drum accompaniment to Walter Gibbons' mixing at Galaxy 21, the Parisian expatriate was seduced by the emerging sound of disco. Soon he took to the decks at clubs like New York New York and the Flamingo, eventually progressing to gigs at Studio 54, Better Days, and even the Loft and Paradise Garage.

Concurrently, François began performing A&R chores at the seminal dance indie Prelude, where he remixed and/or edited countless cuts, including Musique's "(Push Push) In the Bush" and D-Train's "Keep On." As demand for his skills escalated, he retired from DJing in 1983 and began working as a remixer and producer for a phenomenal roster of luminaries: Kraftwerk, Yazoo, Eurythmics, U2, Diana Ross, Mick Jagger, and Depeche Mode (to name a few).

François has remained active throughout the '90s. In 1994, he founded Wave Records, an independent label devoted to cultivating "lasting music with substance as well as style," responsible for such diverse releases as Abstract Truth's "Get Another Plan," Kevin Aviance's number-one cover of "Din Da Da," and François K.'s own "Time & Space." He also continues to remix artists from Cesaria Evora to Juan Atkins.

Since returning to the DJ booth, François has spun at many New York City landmarks (Twilo, Roxy, Sound Factory Bar), and throughout England, Italy, and Japan. In 1996, with partners Joe Claussell and Danny Krivit, he kicked off Body & Soul, a club celebrated for its devoted following and eclectic program, which encompasses the full musical breadth of the seasoned DJ team.

"I think in the future people will have to have an ability to do lots of different things—synthesis as opposed to specialization," remarked François back in 1983. Adding fortune-teller to his list of accomplishments might be overkill, but history has definitely borne out his prescience.

mathèque. Ironically, a film director, Roger Vadim (*Barbarella*) later lay claim to coining the former term. The shortened word *disco* eventually came to mean both the actual spaces and the popular music born within them.

The first notable New York disco, Le Club, opened in 1960. But music was strictly for background ambience at Le Club and similar boîtes that followed. Epitomizing a delicate balance of class and kitsch in presentation, the emphasis in these establishments was on discreet socializing among the upper classes, with a red carpet at the ready for VIPs. In many regards, the same mind-set—music as a secondary concern to celebrities and a select crowd—prevailed even during disco's '70s heyday at Studio 54.

The true spirit of disco, and the roots of the music in even its most mainstream incarnation, lay far beyond the public eye, in clubs that catered squarely to black, gay, and Latin patrons.

> The black gay underground was the key. The gay community is the people who embraced disco wholeheartedly in the first place and helped it become what it is today. Many of the creators, the people who really started all this and made it possible, still aren't being acknowledged.
>
> —François K.

The first such club of note in New York was Salvation, which opened in 1969. DJ Terry Noel's program included funk, Latin, and soul platters but also a hefty dose of rock, spun without interruptions. Rather than fade tracks in and out, DJs were beginning to try to keep the beats going constantly, so the dancers' energy never waned. One night, Noel failed to show up for work. Dancer Francis Grasso, a turntable novice from Brooklyn, filled in; when Noel eventually materialized, he found himself out of a job.

A year later, Francis moved on to the Sanctuary. Originally christened the Church and nestled in Manhattan's Hell's Kitchen section, the club featured a decadent-cum-ecclesiastical décor, complete with stained glass windows and blasphemous depictions of angels in flagrante delicto. Although the club initially catered to a straight white crowd, the new management actively recruited a gay clientele, and the Sanctuary soon became a premiere hot spot for uninhibited homosexuals.

On his turntables atop the altar, Grasso set a new standard for his craft. Sanctuary sets included plenty of soul and R&B, from Memphis sounds like Isaac Hayes and Irma Thomas to Motown and James Brown to early Kool and the Gang. But rock acts like Chicago, the Doors, the Rolling Stones, and even the Beatles were also featured, plus African percussion pieces and extended Latin workouts. Communing closely with his crowd, Grasso—and his alternates, Steve D'Acquisto and Michael Cappello—reabsorbed the excitement his selections generated on the floor, then channeled it back by choosing tracks to intensify or alter the mood.

> Francis had some of the finest taste in music I've ever known. He was the true master of this whole art. We all come from Francis. He was the beginning, the original.
> —Steve D'Acquisto

> Francis was extremely talented. A skinny little Italian kid from Brooklyn, but incredible. He had a very good ear for music. Mixes were coming into play, and music was breaking through into another world.
> —David Mancuso

Grasso's secret weapon in this mass seduction was a technique he'd developed called slip-cueing, which allowed him to stitch records together in longer sequences, creating musical layers. By placing a felt pad between the turntable platter and record, he could hold the latter in place with his finger while the former spun at full speed, unencumbered, beneath. Adjusting the LP or single with his finger while the player kept moving, he'd isolate the perfect point of entry for the next song, then drop it in on top of the music that was already playing.

> You had to really know the records, especially the beginning, because we didn't have headphones back then. Francis would say, "Just listen over [the speakers], because you know what you want to hear, and they're not hearing it yet. They're out there dancing to the previous record, while you're listening deep into the one that's coming in." Most of the records had natural introductions. We'd use a downbeat or a drum roll, and at that point we'd bring it in, on the beat with the other record.
>
> —Steve D'Acquisto

Over time, this practice was further refined. Turntables with pitch control allowed tempos to be sped up or slowed down, so two different records could be in near perfect time with each other. Modest modifications to high-, middle-, and low-range frequencies could be made via equalization (EQ) controls, thus compensating for acoustic losses, amplifying propulsive bass lines, and smoothing out rough patches between elements in a mix.

Eventually, Grasso reached a point where his mixes could last upward of a couple minutes. Splicing the rhythm track of Chicago's "I'm A Man" together with Robert Plant's impassioned panting on Led Zeppelin's "Whole Lotta Love," he anticipated the erotic content of mainstream disco classics by several years.

Grasso, D'Acquisto, Cappello, and others would disseminate these techniques among the city's discos, even after the Sanctuary closed in 1972. Even though he never made a record of his own, Francis Grasso's innovative mixing, his knack for isolating points of intersection between two records to create spontaneous minicompositions, made him the first prominent American DJ to raise his art to an original musical discipline. Adored and lauded by his crowd, he also presaged the trend of DJ-as-

MEET THE DJ

Steve D'Acquisto

Some men are born for the DJ booth; others are thrust into it. "I got started because I was over at Francis [Grasso]'s house," recalls Steve D'Acquisto. Exhausted from two weeks of nonstop work, the Sanctuary legend couldn't face another night. "He said, 'Do you want to go in and play?' I said, 'What the hell do I know about playing records?' 'Just pretend you're me.'"

Grasso's instincts were correct. "It came pretty naturally to me," admits D'Acquisto. "Because I'd watched him, I just understood." From the Sanctuary, D'Acquisto continued on to gigs at Le Jardin and other clubs and was a regular fixture at the Loft. Along with David Mancuso, he launched the New York Record Pool in 1975, using his connections to foster unity within the DJ community.

In 1980, D'Acquisto collaborated with cellist-composer Arthur Russell under the moniker Loose Joints, yielding the classic "Is It All Over My Face" and "Pop Your Funk." Alternate Loose Joints material is slated for inclusion on a forthcoming Russell anthology.

D'Acquisto stopped DJing professionally in 1984, increasingly disillusioned with the focus on seamless mixing by tempo. "There's no power in the way people are stringing things together when you start playing by beats per minute."

"When I retired from being a DJ, I screwed around in the record business, and then took some time off." When he returned to the workplace, D'Acquisto had no problem parlaying his experience into a position with Linn Hi-Fi, UK manufacturer of specialized sound systems. "I travel all over the U.S. and go to Europe about five times a year, too."

And although he no longer spins, D'Acquisto refuses to rule out the possibility. "I would love to do an old-timers' tour, to go out on the road and alternate mixes with David [Mancuso] and Michael Cappello all night. Nicky Siano, too. That would be a lot of fun."

celebrity. (With fame came tragedy, too; after crossing criminal elements at one engagement, he was beaten so severely he required plastic surgery to reconstruct his facial features.)

> If anybody was a real pop star early on, it was Francis. He was the only one. The club owners wanted to clone him.
> —Steve D'Acquisto

But the DJ who would come to define the practice of celebrating the crowd was further downtown, at 647 Broadway, where David Mancuso ran his weekly party, the Loft.

> When it comes to the downtown movement, David Mancuso's the original. Francis Grasso and other people started it, but they did it uptown, in midtown. David's point was hedonistic, the pleasure of dancing, and coming to a place where you can hear the best music on the best sound system, one night a week only.
> —François K.

The Loft (its given name—Mancuso never officially chose one) first opened its doors on Valentine's Day 1970. The mix of music being played didn't vary too much from the fare at the Sanctuary or any of the other underground clubs. What distinguished the Loft was the atmosphere.

> Back in the 1970s and late sixties, there were a lot of things going on. You would go to a civil rights march or a gay liberation [rally] and meet people. I knew a lot of different people. Somebody recently wrote . . . that you might see somebody at the Loft that, if you saw them on the subway, you'd never speak to them. But I knew everybody that came through that door; they just came from different environments.
> —David Mancuso

MEET THE DJ

David Mancuso

Many things have changed since David Mancuso opened the club known as the Loft in 1970. His commitments to music and fellowship, however, aren't among them.

"It was a different world then, the world of flower power, Vietnam, the civil rights movement, hippies, and Timothy Leary's visions of a better world to come," wrote the DJ in a 1999 anniversary letter. "Since then, it has reared an entire generation in song and dance. From the music, we have given birth to a whole generation of friendship and love. It is an enviable record...that has lasted twenty-nine wonderful years...of good, clean, honest fun. We are part of all of you who have made this possible."

In addition to nurturing the Loft through its multiple incarnations on Broadway, Prince Street, and later in exile in the East Village, Mancuso's cooperative philosophy inspired him to launch the New York Record Pool with Steve D'Acquisto in 1975. "I thought to myself, *Car pools—everybody sharing*, so I suggested a record pool. And we took it from there."

In recent years, Mancuso has made several DJ tours of Japan and compiled a two-disc CD anthology, *David Mancuso Presents the Loft*. And the energetic fifty-four-year-old (who was born upstate in Utica) is making preparations to reopen the Loft anew. "I want to make sure I have the right situation," he says of the delays. "I have a few opportunities, but I'm not going to jump." His devotees are willing to wait. "I still have people coming from the beginning, and definitely from at least fifteen years ago. I'm into third-generation [patrons] now. That's amazing, and very rewarding."

In addition to his musical pursuits, Mancuso has served as chairman of the board for the nonprofit Adopt A Building for eight years. "We rehabilitate buildings that the city will give us, fix them up, and create housing for seniors and low-income families. You've got to give back to the community."

> The Loft was very different, because it was a very black, very gay crowd, and it was only one night a week. It was a house party; it lasted from midnight to seven A.M., and that was it. It cost two bucks to get in, and everything inside was free: coat check, spreads of food you couldn't believe, and the best punch you've ever tasted. There was nothing like that punch ever again—and it wasn't spiked.
>
> —Steve D'Acquisto

The crowd was an essential component of the Loft's dynamic—one became a member by invitation only, and guest privileges were limited—but the music and sound were vitally important, too. Mancuso remains devoted to reproducing records in the truest fidelity possible to this day. In both the original Broadway Loft space and later at its second, better-known home at 99 Prince Street, the sound system—which included customized speakers, amplifiers, turntables, and even hand-crafted cartridges—was always the best. Contrary to some reports, the volume was never earsplitting. It didn't have to be.

> David was using very high end stuff. And it was more of a house system than a club system, so it had all the qualities of a great hi-fi, and yet it had punch. It could move a big room. The way he had it laid out was just perfect.
>
> —Steve D'Acquisto

> Every record could stand on its own. I always try to pursue what the artist intended, and that should reach the ear unobtrusively. I like good clean sound.
>
> —David Mancuso

In the beginning, David wasn't mixing. He was just playing one record after another, on two turntables. With some influence from myself, he started to mix. "David," I said, "there really shouldn't be any silence. Keep the party going."

—Steve D'Acquisto

For many years, Mancuso mixed records together in the manner of the Sanctuary DJs. Though headphones still weren't common, he initiated the now-common practice of positioning a monitor by the turntables, so the DJ could gauge the sound of the mix in the speakers without interference from time-delay or room acoustics. Eventually, he decided that eschewing any type of layered mix was truer to his muse.

A record has a beginning point and an end point. I stopped cutting into records, because the mix started becoming too important. The law of averages is you're going to get some right and some wrong. Then you start being judged, and judging yourself, and it becomes this whole thing that has nothing to do with music.

—David Mancuso

Although other clubs had preceded it, the Loft became ground zero for the New York underground dance movement. DJs came to soak up the atmosphere; a young Larry Levan told Mancuso the Loft was "his spiritual home." In time, both Nicky Siano and Levan would attempt to create a similar vibe at their own venues. Entrepreneurs took inspiration from it, too, and the powers behind pivotal clubs like Hurrah, New York New York, and Le Jardin passed through its doors. Regardless of background or intent, visitors to the Loft rarely left unchanged.

It was like walking into never-never land. One of the most vivid memories of my life is walking through that door and hearing the music, seeing the lights. David used theatrical lighting, like set changes using color. David is the [Leonardo] da Vinci of our set, a real master. He saw things in a whole different way.

—Steve D'Acquisto

> I was in New York when the Loft had their twenty-fifth anniversary. It was amazing, like no club I've ever been to. It was a loft space, but it was like a Hawaiian beach. They'd play a track, and let it play right out to the end. Everyone would clap, and then they'd start another track. There was no pretense of mixing. It was twenty-five years of every classic they'd ever played there.
>
> —Ben Dubuisson (Purple Penguin)

In the early '70s there was no codified, easily identified music called disco. The orchestrated R&B of Philadelphia, as represented by producers like Gamble & Huff, and hits like "The Love I Lost" by Harold Melvin & the Blue Notes and "TSOP (The Sound of Philadelpia)" by MFSB featuring the Three Degrees, would become an important element in the sound ultimately dubbed disco. But initially, if a record got played in clubs and people danced to it, that's all it took to make it a disco record.

Slowly, the role of the DJ as a conduit between the music industry and consumers began to emerge. In 1973, Manu Dibango's "Soul Makossa," a platter recorded by an African jazz artist in Paris, went from being an obscure import to a Top 40 hit after extensive exposure via club DJs. The era of the DJ as hitmaker had arrived. By the following year, discos were routinely repeating this pattern, making number-one singles out of both George McRae's "Rock Your Baby" and the Hues Corporation's "Rock the Boat."

> At that point in time, it was more important to play one great record after another after another. Just keep the energy peaked, and have people be entertained, so they'd ask you, "What is that record? I have to get that!" We sold a lot of records.
>
> —Steve D'Acquisto

These trends weren't lost on the record companies, or their artists. By 1975, the dawn of the mainstream craze, tracks such as Van McCoy's "Do the Hustle" and Donna Summer's "Love to Love You, Baby" were being composed specifically with disco patrons in mind. The latter, originally recorded with a running time suited for airplay, was soon extended into a sixteen-plus-minute opus of erotic moans and repetitive, synthesizer-driven minimalism, after the party guests of Casablanca Records' Neil Bogart responded so enthusiastically he had to keep replaying the track.

> A lot of the music was on 45s. We lived for long records hot enough to keep people on the floor, like [the Rolling Stones'] "Sympathy for the Devil"—that's six or seven minutes. The whole idea of doing a remix was to take a great piece of music and make it more interesting and longer...a record that had peaks and valleys.
>
> —Steve D'Acquisto

To meet the increasing demands of disco DJs, record companies responded in 1975 with a new format: the twelve-inch maxi single. Manufactured at LP size, but pressed to be played at 45 rpm like a traditional, seven-inch single, these individual tracks could run up to fifteen minutes in length. And because the grooves weren't as narrow, the fidelity was markedly improved.

DJs and producers quickly recognized the medium as an ideal outlet for extended, enhanced versions of popular tracks. The people who ran the decks knew what kind of music thrilled their disciples and what specifically within a track really clicked. Now DJs could refurbish tracks with their own input, creating something greater than the sum of the individual parts, and commit the outcome to permanent posterity. This new incarnation was dubbed the remix.

> Take a record like [Dennis Coffey's] "Scorpio," which had this fantastic drum beat. We'd always mix it back and forth, take a really good break, and make it longer. That's where a twelve-inch came into play. The record companies could take a record and extend it and give the people what they wanted.
>
> —David Mancuso

The idea of the remix is originally credited to producer Tom Moulton, who was remixing cuts by the Trammps as early as 1972. But Moulton's vision was limited by the confines of the seven-inch (his remixes often appeared as b sides). Although he did toy with melodic elements and percussive passages, his priority was calibrating individual tracks in a recording for maximum impact with dancers.

It was Walter Gibbons who crafted the first truly revolutionary twelve-inch remix. As a live DJ, Gibbons was renown for his versatile mixing style. He could maintain a groove under even the slowest of intros with his deft edits; stretch percussive breaks by cutting back and forth between records; and phase songs, playing two copies simultaneously to create a woozy sonic trail. Applying these concepts to Double Exposure's "Ten Percent," he overhauled the original until it lasted almost ten propulsive minutes. Released on the Salsoul label, it was the first commercially available twelve-inch.

Spurred to even wider public acceptance by the 1977 hit film *Saturday Night Fever*, disco became a national phenomenon. But while movie's multiplatinum soundtrack included genuine knockouts (most notably the Trammps' "Disco Inferno"), to suburban Americans it was the lighter fare from the Bee Gees and KC and the Sunshine Band that became synonymous with disco. Although this subculture had launched formidable artists like Sylvester and Chic into the limelight, the airwaves and record stores became glutted with a barrage of thin soundalikes from both bewildered stars and hopeful neophytes. Radio stations converted to all-disco formats to handle the slew of interchangeable material. The clichè beat now masquerading as disco was used to anchor everything from Beethoven to the "I Love Lucy" theme, and even made Rick Dees' moronic "Disco Duck" the number-one record in the country (for a sole week, mercifully).

Frank Sinatra and Ethel Merman were making disco records. Everybody wanted to have a disco hit, because disco was selling like crazy. Disco became the boat that everybody wanted to jump in. It was the era of greed in the music industry. The record companies were the heaviest, and the first to jump in...and they sunk the whole boat.

—Steve D'Acquisto

By 1977, there were over 10,000 discothèques in America. Every bar that fell on hard times decided that a disco makeover would afford salvation. Amidst all the media hype—The Clothes! The Dancing! The Stars!—outstanding music and its power to move people, which had spawned the craze in the first place, shuffled in the shadows.

This shift is particularly evident in the legacy of Studio 54. Opened in April 1977, the club epitomized the high life to disco devotees, with its elaborate parties, glamorous celebrities, and clamoring throng at the entrance. Yet although the world looked to this establishment as a standard-bearer, history rarely treats its music or the DJ's role there with the same regard afforded other clubs, before or after, considered highly influential.

In all the books, press, and movies about Studio 54, nobody ever mentions Richie Kaczor, the main DJ. Every time I heard him play, I was in awe of how smooth he was. He was able to accommodate a very cosmopolitan, international crowd. He was a turntable artist, but not somebody that everybody knows about, because he never made any records. But there's a difference between being involved in making successful records and being a really great DJ.

—François K.

People didn't go to Studio 54 for the music. They went to Studio 54 to be seen and party and do drugs and socialize. Studio 54 was a great club, and they had really good DJs and a fabulous sound system. And I enjoyed the music there. But you didn't go to Studio because you knew the DJ was going to do profound, earth-moving stuff.

—Peter Calandra

There was that faction of people who went to 54 to be seen, and then there was a whole other faction of people who went there to dance, just like everyplace else. You couldn't really get away from the music at 54.

—Steve D'Acquisto

But by 1979, an oversaturated American public had reached its fill of disco. That summer, Chicago's Comiskey Park, home of baseball's White Sox, was rocked by a midgame antidisco record-burning rally. *Can't Stop the Music*, the film vehicle engineered for chart-toppers the Village People, proved an embarrassing flop of epic proportions. The bottom of the market had completely fallen out. When the hits dried up, the record labels slashed dance departments and scrambled to change tack.

Disco and the diehards that had nurtured it simply returned to the underground, their numbers now fortified by new fans that had seen past the glitter to the heart of the music. Even as the good ship *Disco* was sinking out of the nation's embittered view, the stage was being set for the genre's maturation, down on King Street in Soho, at a club dubbed the Paradise Garage, in the hands of a DJ named Larry Levan.

Larry was a real sweetheart, and he loved music. He was one with the people. He had that certain contact with them. He was one of the earlier DJs, out there from a long time ago, and that's where his crowd came from. He was trusted and respected by the people who came [to Paradise Garage] to dance.

—David Mancuso

Larry Levan was born and raised in Brooklyn. He was instilled with a love for blues, jazz, and gospel by his mother at a young age;

35

by his teens, he'd already learned about mixing, inspired by the promise of music that never ends. The Paradise Garage wasn't the first club where he'd played music. He'd cut his teeth at the infamous Continental Baths (the gay bathhouse that launched Bette Midler), SoHo Place, and Reade Street. The Paradise Garage, however, would be his Shangri-la, a kingdom where for the bulk of the '80s he exhorted 2,000-plus dancers nightly to surrender themselves to his eclectic selections and all-encompassing sound system.

Levan had designed the latter in tandem with Richard Long (who owned the lower Broadway loft—sound familiar?—that had housed SoHo Place and built equipment for Mancuso). The DJ was notorious for spending hours checking for sonic gaps and inconsistencies every week, even leaving patrons to wait outside while adjustments were made immediately before opening. Where Mancuso was a fanatic about pristine, unaltered sound, Levan manipulated every aspect, adding completely new dimensions to the records he played, hitting the dancers on a subconscious but very physical level, with tweaked highs and rumbling lows.

> At the Garage, I could only be in the room behind the floor, or up in the booth. I could never be on the floor, because Larry used to hurt me with the bass. He would pin me to the wall sometimes. It was really loud in there.
>
> —Steve D'Acquisto

The music he programmed bore his distinctive stamp, too. He helped popularize underground black classics like "Moody" by ESG, and "Time Warp" by reggae singer Eddy Grant. He pushed boundaries, throwing tracks like Van Halen's "Jump" into the mix. Like many of his peers, he often wove a series of songs into a narrative or connected them by sentiment, so a song like "Music" by Al Hudson might dovetail with "I Love Music" by the O'Jays. When Levan finished such a suite, he wasn't averse to using an extended silence to punctuate the pause before moving on.

MEET THE DJ

Peter Calandra

Peter Calandra

Growing up in New York in the '70s, Peter Calandra—purveyor of "authentic Manhattan-style '70s soul, funk, and disco"—fell in love with music via the radio. In his late teens, he came out of the closet and immediately became an ardent denizen of the city's key discos: "the original Limelight, Studio 54, Ice Palace, Infinity, Flamingo, 12 West...and the Anvil."

Soon he started buying twelve-inch singles. He paid close attention to the playlists of the DJs he admired—men like Robbie Leslie, Jim Burgess, and Roy Thode—and sought out the same tracks. "I was so into the music that when I would hear a version of a record at a club like 12 West, every six minutes I was running up to Jim Burgess, asking, 'What's the name of this?'"

Inevitably, Peter befriended the men that moved him. Meanwhile his library of vinyl was climbing into the thousands. "Without even realizing it, when I was starting to collect these records, I had intent," he admits today. Purchasing his own equipment, he tried to apply the musical lessons he'd learned on the dance floor to developing a uniquely personal programming style. By the time he left New York in 1981, the DJs he'd grown up with were tapping him to fill in when they needed a night off.

Relocated in San Diego, he worked steadily throughout the '80s at several popular gay bars. There he attracted a clique of dedicated followers who appreciated his special commitment to preserving "morning music," the lush, slower sets that New York and circuit party DJs typically saved till dawn's early light.

Today, Calandra lives in Seattle, captivating young patrons who missed disco's heyday with a sophisticated sensibility that comes only with experience. "You want brain surgery, you go to a brain surgeon," he says with smile. "You want disco? Go to a forty-year-old DJ from New York, not someone who's twenty-eight and collecting '90s music. It's not rocket science."

Larry Levan once said to me, "Nobody would understand that you and I are exactly the same kind of DJ, because all they hear is the music, and our tastes sound totally different. But we both talk to and play with our audience. We fuck with their minds, but they understand that it's just communication. We'll stop the music. We don't match beats. We'll take them to a point, and they think they know where they're going, and then we'll take them in a completely different direction."

—Anita Sarko

[Larry] had unique, one-of-a-kind chemistry with his audience. With another audience, he would have been a huge failure. He got away with things that I would have been fired for—just letting records fade out and having dead air for any amount of time. Whether that was accidental or part of some incredibly sophisticated scheme, I don't know. But in my limited exposure, I saw enough to realize he was a combination of a savant, a real genius...and a spoiled baby.

—Robbie Leslie

Levan's ability to communicate through music connected with his admirers in a profound manner, inspiring devotion on par with attendees of the Loft. Paradise Garage had a strict door policy, and memberships were difficult to obtain; gay members could attend either night on weekends, but straight patrons were barred from predominantly gay Saturdays. Unlike Mancuso, Levan had financial backing, a bigger space, and—most significantly—a desire to be in the public eye. Such celebrities as Mick Jagger, Mike Tyson, and Boy George passed through the doors; pop artist Keith Haring and singer Grace Jones were regular fixtures. Because Levan came to the attention of more people, the ripples of his influence spread further; the emotional bond with his crowd was indisputable.

Levan also left a deep mark on DJ culture and pop music via his work in the recording studio. Many records he remixed remain classics in the canon: Gwen Guthrie's "Ain't Nothin' Goin' on but the Rent," Class Action's "Weekend," Taana Gardner's "Heartbeat" and "Work That Body," Loose Joints' "Is It All Over My Face." Blessed with a keen ear, Levan imparted tracks with extra gravity without compromising their swing, amplifying and extending the intensity of the originals. His spacey aural constructions are often reminiscent of those of dub reggae innovators like King Tubby. As producer and musical collaborator with the Peech Boys ("Don't Make Me Wait," "Life Is Something Special"), he took his musical ideas even further, fusing soulful vocals with studio trickery and inventive electronics.

When the Paradise Garage closed its doors in September 1987, Levan became a nomad. As Robbie Leslie surmised, his distinctive approach never quite connected with the audiences he later played for at clubs like the World and Palladium. Meanwhile, his prodigious drug consumption, unreliable working habits, and knack for running up studio costs hurt his reputation with record companies. In November 1992, shortly after completing a two-month DJ tour of Japan, Larry Levan (who'd been born with a heart condition) died of endocarditis, an inflammation of the heart's lining. But the influence of his spirit on DJs and music lovers resonates to this day.

> The Garage opened my eyes to the future of club music. I don't think I'd be where I am now if I hadn't gone there. It was that influential. There wasn't a vibe in British clubs at the same time. Here it was all about what you wore and how you looked. In Paradise Garage it was all about the music, the sound system, and the dancing.
>
> —Paul Oakenfold

Although mainstream America and major record labels thought disco was long buried, the music continued to flourish throughout the '80s, albeit in a variety of diverse strains reminiscent of its eclectic origins. Branching out into signing and grooming artists for record labels, production, and songwriting, as well as remixing, DJs like François K., Walter Gibbons, Shep Pettibone, and Mark Kamins further advanced the art. John "Jellybean" Benitez, who electrified crowds of thousands of black, Latin, and Italian kids at the Funhouse, eventually trumped Francis for the title First Celebrity DJ with his successful productions and highly publicized romance with a new star named Madonna.

Incorporating elements of rap and later the nascent Chicago house sound, the music mutated further, and new terms were coined for each genre: *freestyle, electro,* and even *garage* (a term as elastic as the original *disco*). The names changed, but the beat continued uninterrupted. There's no need to go retrieve Dad's white polyester leisure suit from Goodwill, but disco never really died.

> Dancing was the first form of self-expression, even before words. People always dance to things that have a beat. Call it whatever you want to—disco or swing or jazz—it's still dance music. From the Original Dixieland Jazz Band right on up to Monica, it's the same thing. Nobody's ever going to kill dance music. They may change the name of it...but it's nothing but disco.
>
> —Steve D'Acquisto

MEET THE DJ

Robbie Leslie

Some DJs start with piano lessons. Others riffle through their parents' records. But Florida's Robbie Leslie didn't have any inkling about music as a youth. "None whatsoever," he laughs. "My family wasn't musically inclined. There was rarely even a radio on in the house or car." As a teenager, he discovered Motown and soul and later, classical, two incongruous styles that dovetailed perfectly when he began spinning disco.

But when Leslie accepted a job at a club on New York's infamous Fire Island, he still didn't have big aspirations. "I started as a waiter, then was bumped up to bartender." After the summer season, the club stopped hiring DJs. Leslie offered to fill in for free. "Once I started, it was like heroin. I was instantly hooked."

In 1979, he moved to Manhattan to go pro. His dramatic mixing style made him a big hit with the crowds at the seminal club 12 West...until the following autumn. "The Saint opened in September of 1980, and the following weekend, 12 West was on the verge of closing."

Fortunately, the Saint knew a good thing when they heard one, and they hired Leslie immediately. "Christmas 1980, was my first day playing there. It was quite a present." For the next six years, he remained a top draw, making the Saint a New York landmark and a mandatory stop for gay travelers.

In November 1986, he left the Saint. "I'd watched the first string of serious mixing DJs slowly but surely take less prestigious gigs, and I got scared. I was riding this crest that I knew couldn't go on for forever, and I thought, *This is a good time to reevaluate*. I decided to leave New York and get out of the business."

Leslie returned to Florida but couldn't stay in retirement. These days, he continues to spin at circuit parties, club dates in Miami, and even regular cruise ship gigs. Old habits are hard to break.

3 Dance to the Drummer's Beat

Although disco was already in rapid decline when hip-hop music—or, as it was called back then, rap—first surfaced in the record stores in 1979, the genres share more traits in common than average campers realize. Distinctly urban in character, the two sounds had evolved concurrently throughout the '70s.

There were distinct differences, of course. In big-city discos, replacing a house band with a DJ was a question of economy. Conversely, the Bronx was riddled with poverty and troubled by gangs and drug abuse. Since instruments and instruction were an unaffordable luxury, relying on records and turntables for music was a practice born of necessity. But because hip-hop first took shape in the Bronx, far away from the major label record companies (and posh discos) of midtown Manhattan, it remained an isolated phenomenon much longer.

Just like *Saturday Night Fever*, the earliest musical export from the hip-hop community to cross over to middle America wasn't entirely authentic. Even though it was originally only released as a twelve-inch single, "Rapper's Delight" by the Sugarhill Gang was the first rap track to enter *Billboard*'s prestigious Hot 100 chart, peaking at number thirty-six in the first week of 1980. With bubbling rhymes bobbing atop a bass riff lifted directly from "Good Times," Chic's number-one single from the summer before, the track proved irrepressibly catchy.

Never mind that the Sugarhill Gang had been fabricated at a savvy producer's behest for the sole purpose of cutting a record, or that this wasn't even the first commercially released rap track (that was 1979's "King Tim III [Personality Jock]" by Fatback). Many listeners quickly dismissed rap as a novelty anyway. Had they witnessed firsthand the pioneers who'd been nurturing hip-hop for six years, they might have been alarmed to see how closely this new sound's growth paralleled that of disco, the music they'd just turned their backs on. Both cultures had blossomed deep in the underground, and, much more importantly, the innovations of DJs lay at their creative core.

> Kool Herc was the father. He brought the sound of the break-beats, playing records like "The Mexican" by Babe Ruth and "Apache"—what they would call "The Rock"—by the Incredible Bongo Band.
>
> —Afrika Bambaataa

The story of hip-hop music begins with a young man named Clive Campbell, alias Hercules, who earned the nickname thanks to his muscular physique. Later he shortened his moniker to Herc, and his graffiti tag was Kool Herc. Although Campbell's family had lived in the Bronx since 1967, he was born in Kingston, Jamaica, in 1955.

Herc's heritage played an essential role in the emergence of hip-hop. In Jamaica, traveling sound systems operated by DJs had been an entertainment staple since the close of World War II. American R&B had taken root with the island natives, but since recreating the sounds live eluded local musicians (who typically traded in tourist-oriented calypso fare), playing records over enormous loudspeakers was an easier solution. Since the music had to penetrate large assemblies of dancers, bass was an important priority, and speaker cabinets of ludicrous proportions were common.

Typically, more than one sound system would be invited to a

party, and crews would battle via volume and song selection; the DJs who emerged victorious became stars. In turn, they began producing original records, geared specifically toward pleasing dancers. Shuffling rhythms and booming bass were paramount, and though various styles—ska, rock steady, reggae—evolved over the decades, DJs remained pivotal in the creation and popularization of each.

Herc's first DJ gig of note was a birthday party for his sister in 1973. Encouraged by the enthusiastic response he received, Herc began playing at block parties, in parks, and in schools throughout the Bronx, transporting his gear in one of the earliest coffins (a case for storing two turntables and a mixer). Noticing that Jamaican music typically failed to generate the same crowd reaction it had back home, Herc generously peppered his sets with harder sounds, heavy on the funk and Latin jams. An avid music lover, his tastes were further informed by disco DJs with roots in the Bronx, including Grandmaster Flowers and Pete DJ Jones, who regularly spun cuts that became seminal in the hip-hop canon, such as James Brown's "Give It Up or Turn It Loose."

Although the aesthetics of disco figured into the mentality of early hip-hop DJs, the tunes they played were a reaction to the increasingly streamlined R&B sound that dominated the airwaves.

> [Record companies] were just shoving disco down our throats. For the first two years, we were playing it, and that was cool. But the dancers in the black and Latino community change every three months. Then after the third and fourth year, they were trying to get rid of the funk. You weren't hearing James [Brown] and Sly [and the Family Stone] on the radio much, so to keep the audiences kicking with the funk, we started adding all their stuff, and other funky beats, to our musical repertoire.
>
> —Afrika Bambaataa

Aside from his programming tastes, Kool DJ Herc's contributions

MEET THE DJ

Kurtis Mantronik of Mantronix

As a youth in Canada, Jamaican-born Kurtis Mantronik's musical fantasies were remarkably commonplace. "I remember going to school dances, where a local band would play, and I'd think, *I want to get a guitar, because it's cool.*"

His definition of *cool* changed markedly when the family relocated to New York and his cousins exposed him to block parties in the Bronx. He absorbed what he witnessed and taught himself how to DJ on a system cobbled together from discarded stereo parts. (Unfortunately, he didn't get the wiring quite right, so he occasionally got burned when his cuing earphone overheated.) All thoughts of playing guitar were abandoned. "I got two turntables and a beat-box," he grins. "That's how I started."

As rap entered the mainstream, detractors dismissed it as a fad. Kurtis knew better. "From being in that lifestyle, I understood a form of music that I knew could one day be big."

In the early '80s, he worked at the now defunct Downtown Records, saving his wages and DJ fees until he had enough cash—a whopping eighty dollars—to produce his first track, "Fresh Is the Word." The tune landed him a deal, and a string of classics followed, climaxing with the widely sampled "King of the Beats." As *DJ* magazine noted, Mantronik continued where Afrika Bambaataa's "Planet Rock" left off, "injecting further musical depth and programming into hip-hop."

During most of the '90s, Kurtis kept a low profile. But recently, he's returned to the fray on every front. His remixes for Future Sound of London ("We Have Explosives") and BT ("Love, Peace and Grease") introduced him to a new generation of dance music fans, and his 1998 *I Sing the Body Electro* found him in surprisingly fresh form. And although he may not be filling in for an ailing X-ecutioner soon, he still knows how to pump a party. "I can't do everything anymore," he winks, "but I can still do some stuff."

to the legacy of hip-hop were twofold. First, to pump up both the assembled crowds and his own reputation, Herc amplified his jams with oversize speakers dubbed "Herculoids," reminiscent of the sound systems from his youth.

Most important, Herc recognized what it took to keep a party rocking and he concentrated on isolating the stripped-down percussion passages of his records, which sounded especially good over the Herculoids and upped the excitement. Rather than spin a record in its entirety, he'd tease the crowd with these "breaks," alternating between two especially hot platters or extending a break even further by playing two copies, one after the other. Witnessed by youngsters at parties in the parks, the practice soon caught on.

> You had to have two copies of the same record, so when the groove came up and it was about to run out, you'd throw on the other [copy] and start it over again.
>
> —Kurtis Mantronik

In pursuit of more and better breaks, he combed record store bargain bins searching for tracks that contained such percussive peaks, like "Listen to Me" by Baby Huey, or "Scorpio" by Dennis Coffey & the Detroit Guitar Band (also a fave with disco jocks). His signature tune was a cover of the Shadows' instrumental hit "Apache," albeit as whipped into a rhythmic spaghetti-Western frenzy by Michael Viner's Incredible Bongo Band.

> The whole key was finding the records nobody had, breaks and beats people weren't playing, just to see the shock on everybody's face if you played something new. Now you can go down to your local record shop and they've got twenty of the greatest beats on one album.
>
> —Prince Paul

MEET THE DJ

Prince Paul

Not all mercurial musicians named Prince behave like nutcases. For over a decade, Prince Paul has helped craft countless records cherished by pop and hip-hop fans. His latest is *So . . . How's Your Girl?* by Handsome Boy Modeling School, his collaboration with Dan the Automater. Even though his back catalog may read like a multiple personality disorder case study (he did title an album *Psychoanalysis*), the former Paul Huston remains down-to-earth.

Even before he emerged as the power behind the throne on De La Soul's 1989 debut *3 Feet High and Rising*, Paul had been in the public eye spinning for Stetsasonic, the original hip-hop live band. "DJing has always been my first love," says the Long Island native. Paul first started getting busy on the decks back in the late '70s. Fortunately, he had plenty of opportunities to refine his tricks. "There were probably more block parties on Long Island than in the five boroughs," he insists. "Hard to believe, but there were a ton of DJs back in the day."

The drive to entertain a crowd that informed his sets is reflected in his production style, distinguished by a fondness for old school grooves, giddy samples, and an undercurrent of funk. These days, Prince Paul's résumé as an artist-producer reads like a syllabus for Forward-Thinking Hip-Hop 101: De La Soul, Cypress Hill, Big Daddy Kane, 3rd Bass, Gravediggaz.

After an extended spell away from the decks, Paul resumed DJing a couple years ago. In addition to regular New York gigs, he took his crate of classic beats and contemporary gems out on the road in 1999 to promote his album *A Prince Among Thieves*. His return to the wheels of steel makes as much sense as every other musical decision he's made.

"I never sat down going, 'I'm going to be a DJ,'" the Prince concedes. "I never planned on making records. My approach to everything is carefree and experimental. Because I have a feeling [that] once I start plotting things out, my career's going to end."

Herc's breakbeats inspired a new form of movement, too, dubbed breakdancing. Popping and locking their limbs, heads, and torsos, breakdancers echoed the cut-up music of the DJ with their bodies, mixing old steps with new ones. Spreading out oversize pieces of cardboard or perhaps an abandoned sheet of linoleum, dancers gathered around in a circle, showing off tricks like the helicopter (spinning on one's head) in the center. Along with graffiti painting and DJing, and later rapping, breakdancing was one of the four elemental disciplines that composed hip-hop culture. Those in the life became known as b-boys and b-girls.

To a lesser extent, Herc also helped lay the foundations of rapping, the practice of rhythmically reeling off an extended rhyme to a beat. Taking his style from the rapid-fire patter of black American radio DJs and from toasting, the rhythmic patois practiced by Jamaican DJs, Herc sprinkled his sets with outbursts over the microphone. His assistant, Coke La Rock, picked up the practice, too, adding to Herc's mixes with his lyrical spiel of pop phrases and colloquialisms. But the DJ remained the center of attention.

> Back in those days, DJs were more diverse. You would DJ for a group and for MCs. You DJed on your own, as well as doing tricks. You had to control a party and keep people dancing. Now DJs have specialties, but back then you had to do everything to keep it moving.
>
> —Prince Paul

Inspired by Herc's precedent, DJs began springing up throughout the Bronx. Setting up decks and speakers in parks and schoolyards, they'd juice up their systems with electricity pirated from streetlights. Through battles judged by similar criteria to their Jamaican predecessors, contenders vied for neighborhood supremacy. Within five years, four definitive DJs staked claim to various corners of the Bronx: DJ Breakout (of the Funky Four) in the northernmost regions; Herc in the west; Afrika Bambaataa along the Bronx River east; and in the central and southern sections, Grandmaster Flash. Both Bambaataa and Flash would go on to achieve fame as recording artists, but their early contributions to hip-hop are equally remarkable.

> From a DJ's point of view, Flash was a major influence, how he could mix and cut various different records, but as a collection, a rock record next to a soul record next to an old school hip-hop record. He was a huge part of the setup for me.
>
> —Paul Oakenfold

Grandmaster Flash, alias Joseph Saddler, began spinning shortly after Kool DJ Herc, in 1974. Thanks to his father's expansive record collection, Flash already enjoyed a solid knowledge of music. And as a consequence of his course of studies in electrical engineering at a vocational high school, he was in a unique position to overcome certain technical hurdles despite tight finances.

Having closely observed both Herc and Pete Jones in action, Flash aimed to meld their distinct approaches into his own while overcoming what he perceived as their limitations. His goal was to take Herc's mastery of the breakbeat and match it with Jones's seamless, fluid mixing.

Besting his first obstacle was easy enough, and although Herc would later mock his setup in public, Flash cobbled together his very own sound system. The next step was trickier. After persistent pestering, Pete Jones finally let Flash check out his mixer. With his expertise, the young DJ quickly figured out how Jones had mastered his flawless transitions—the mixer was rigged so cuts could be cued, in the headphones only, before making the segue. Kool Herc, on the other hand, still worked like downtown disco DJs, using the actual speakers as his monitor. Flash quickly customized his own equipment with this feature and was then prepared to take mixing to a new level.

Sharpening his technique through experimentation and practice,

Flash not only learned to keep breaks rolling longer but he could also mix them so smoothly that the transitions flowed right over the crowd. Manipulating the records by hand, he developed backspinning, quickly pulling the record back then letting it spin again, so a word or musical moment could be repeated. And with his modified mixer, he could execute this trick either audibly, creating a rhythmic sound effect, or silently, flicking a switch momentarily to eliminate the sound from the speakers, and then returning it when he let the record go.

To facilitate this trick with utmost speed, he came up with the clock theory, where he identified each record's key components via their relation to the printed label; if he was looking for a specific break on a platter, he knew to cue up to the five o'clock position, for example. In time, other DJs would adopt the practice, using bits of colored tape or labels to mark breaks or phrases.

A third practice he popularized was punch phrasing. Rather than mate two breaks together, Flash would take a break from one song and drop it into the record that continued uninterrupted on the other deck. Gauging the reaction of the crowd, he could select a break—hard or groovy—that would build the mood while adding new contours to the musical passage.

> That's one of the first thing I learned on my own. I would mix an a cappella vocal and just drop in a beat over it, and they would be locked in.
>
> —Kurtis Mantronik

Flash's best-known contribution to hip-hop eventually became a musical discipline unto itself: scratching, the root of contemporary turntablism (sit tight—we'll get there). But although the Grandmaster refined, advanced, and promoted this skill, he didn't actually discover it. Another DJ, Grand Wizard Theodore (who later spun for rap crew the Fantastic Five), did.

Theodore Livingston was the younger brother of Flash's buddy Gene. Flash stored his gear at the Livingstons' pad, and though Gene warned his sibling to keep his hands off, his excitement got the better of him. Flash caught wind of Theodore's enthusiasm and encouraged him.

According to legend, one afternoon in '77 or '78 Theodore, approximately age thirteen at the time, was home practicing when Mrs. Livingston interrupted him. Not wanting to lose track of the groove he'd cued up, he held the record in place, absentmindedly moving it back and forth while listening to his mother. Enchanted by this strange sound in his headphones, he kept practicing, trying to integrate the noise of the needle dragging back and forth across the record into the mix as a musical element.

The more advanced Flash soon picked up on this scratching technique and introduced it to his stylistic repertory, treating a single word like *good* from Chic's "Good Times" as a percussive hit to be manipulated, just like a drum rhythm. Documented on vinyl a few years later, scratching sparked an epiphany in young DJs around the world.

> I was into the club scene before I'd ever heard a hip-hop record. So for instance, I would have heard "Good Times" by Chic as a complete record. All of a sudden Grandmaster Flash was just taking the best bit of a disco record I was into before and making it sound incredibly better than it was originally.
>
> —Andy Smith

Flash's electrical skills also spawned a device called the beatbox. At a few downtown discos like the Electric Circus, a live drummer played along with the DJ and filled in any gaps in the program by keeping a beat going. Flash came up with a mechanized alternative. He took a primitive Vox analog drum machine, designed for storing a few simple percussion patterns, and made it another component in

MEET THE DJ

Andy Smith of Portishead

Most job counselors would consider following in the footsteps of men named Cheese, Flash, and Scratch about as sound as taking career advice from the Seven Dwarves. But for England's Andy Smith, they were the role models who helped make him the success he is today. As warmup DJ for chart-topping trip-hop ensemble Portishead ("Sour Times"), he's pumped up audiences internationally with his mix of film soundtracks, funk, jazz, and—most importantly—top-shelf hip-hop.

"The first time I saw a scratch DJ live was when Kurtis Blow came to this country," he recalls. "Christmas Rapping" and "The Breaks" had done well enough in the United Kingdom to warrant a Bristol date, and Andy was there. "DJ Scratch was on the turntables. I wasn't even looking at Kurtis Blow. My eyes were on the decks behind him, [and I was] thinking, *My God, I'm actually watching somebody do this!*"

Prior to discovering rap, Smith had amassed a substantial collection of New York underground disco. While his classmates bought the latest rock LPs, Andy sought to round out his catalog of Prelude and West End titles, and he kept his ear pressed to Radio Luxembourg to hear mix shows. But once he'd heard what Grandmaster Flash had done to Chic's "Good Times," his fate was sealed.

Andy honed his chops, playing Top 40 in a local nightclub and making amateur hip-hop tapes to sell to local aficionados. He met Geoff Barrow while spinning at a youth club, and the two struck up a friendship. Barrow had a sampler and decks but little vinyl; Smith turned him on to a variety of sounds to sample, helping to lay the foundation for the distinctive audio collage that eventually brought Portishead worldwide recognition.

In 1998, responding to a bootlegged Boston radio set in circulation, Smith released his own album, *The Document*, a mix compilation of tracks by artists including the Jungle Brothers, Marvin Gaye, Peggy Lee, and Jeru the Damaja.

his sound system. Using the beatbox, he augmented the rhythmic palette of his sets even further.

Because Flash brought so many new ideas and devices to the art of the DJ, his contribution to the evolution of rapping comes as an amusing, but important, footnote. Not content to simply execute all the skills he'd mastered hunched over the decks, Flash emerged as a captivating performer, spinning with his hands behind his back or moving records with his feet or head. Between the combination of this showboating, plus the radical sounds he was generating, folks had a habit of stopping the dancing to gather around and watch.

But Flash wasn't trying to lead a school for scratching; he wanted the partygoers to keep moving. He noticed that when his friend Keith Wiggins (later rechristened Cowboy) got on the microphone, he could command the crowd with his playful rhymes. Wiggins would shout, "If you like the sounds that are goin' down, somebody say, 'Oh, yeah.'" And a rousing "Oh yeah!" came bouncing right back. Plus, Cowboy's inventive patter could keep up with Flash's quick changes and dexterous edits. Wiggins quickly became a regular fixture in the Grandmaster's shows and the earliest member of his expanded rap ensemble the Furious Five.

While Flash bolstered the technical legacy of hip-hop significantly, Afrika Bambaataa advanced it along more esoteric and extramusical angles. Although Bambaataa was also a fan of select downtown DJs like Pete Jones, his tastes transcended the programming limits of his hip-hop and disco peers.

> I've got to give props to my mother. When I was growing up, I used to hear James Brown and Motown and the Stax/Watts sound. But then she had the Rolling Stones, the Beatles, and Edith Piaf, and Barbra Streisand. And also African music, like Miriam Makeba, and a lot of West Indian music like the Mighty Sparrow and Harry Belafonte. I was into all types of music.
> —Afrika Bambaataa

At Flash's gigs, audiences were bowled over by the DJ's technical wizardry and showmanship. With "the Master of Records"—Bambaataa—it was the abrupt and zany musical transitions that freed their mind so their ass could follow. Not only did an eclectic collection and ability to make connections between diverse styles secure Bambaataa's reputation as a leading DJ, it also helped create a sense of historical continuity within the emerging pantheon of hip-hop music.

> People that came to Afrika Bambaataa had to be progressive minded. They were going to hear a lot of weird, mind-blowing shit. I might play a commercial, like Coca-Cola's "I'd Like to Teach the World to Sing," and they'd be buggin'. Or I'd say, "I want you to hear what rap used to sound like back in the day," and then take 'em back to the '60s with "The Name Game" or "The Clapping Song" by Shirley Ellis, or "Here Comes the Judge" by Pigmeat Markham. I had a vision, trying to keep people aware as well as having fun.
>
> —Afrika Bambaataa

> We DJed with Afrika Bambaataa once. We went on after him. People kept saying, "Do you want to play records now?" We said, "Oh no; just let him go. He'll decide when he's finished. We'll just sit back here and watch."
>
> —Tom Rowlands (Chemical Brothers)

Competition among DJs was fierce, and the records in one's crate were a closely guarded secret. Toward this end, many DJs started obliterating the printed information on them. In Jamaica, sound-system DJs dogged by similar concerns had soaked off labels in water, a practice adopted by Grandmaster Flash and others in the Bronx. Despite all these preventative measures, rival DJs often managed to divine titles anyway, by stealth, deduction, or intuition.

There was a famous place called Downstairs Records. People used to be in there, watching to see what I was buying. But I was into many different types of music. I might have heard something from the Hare Krishna I want to pick up. So even though it had a beat, it wasn't a [break]beat. But people started buying it. "We know this is a beat!" I said, "Don't buy what I buy, because not everything is a beat.' "

—Afrika Bambaataa

I was so into finding the records the DJs had, and they kept it such a big secret back then. They'd cover [the title] up, soak off the labels. I still have things that are inked out, scratched out. I used to change the covers. Some DJs weren't too bright—they'd blotch out the labels, but in the back [of their crate] you could see the covers up and then you'd know what the record was.

—Prince Paul

Sometimes, if I heard something from another DJ, like Flash or Herc, all I had to do was look at the color of the record to go, "Oh, that's on Polydor" or one of the independent companies. But they had to send their agents to spy on my records, so I'd cover 'em up. They had to wait until I'd played a record for a couple of months, and then I'd start letting the name out.

—Afrika Bambaataa

It's ironic, because when you're DJing, you're trying to expose everybody to whatever songs you've personally found. But in the early hip-hop culture, there were certain people [who] exposed the songs and other people [who] would just bite somebody else's whole set.

—Peanut Butter Wolf

Bambaataa was also the first to appreciate the role of the DJ as a

MEET THE DJ

Kevin Westenburg

Chemical Brothers

They made a single ("Setting Sun") that went number one in England and unclogged the ossified arteries of American rock radio. Their *Dig Your Own Hole* was the first album in the genre dubiously dubbed electronica to attain gold sales status (500,000 copies) on U.S. soil. Their DJ sets pack dive bars and thousand-seat venues alike to the rafters. Even fussy old Boy George adores them. Oh, and they won a Grammy.

Not bad for a pair of dodgy-looking blokes who met studying a remarkably unsexy subject: history. But any college classmates who mistakenly envisioned Tom Rowlands and Ed Simons running around in medieval drag on weekends now know far better. Few duos rock the party as hard as the Chemical Brothers.

Tom and Ed first bonded circa 1990 over shared tastes: hip-hop, techno, house, and American rock. Banging their brand of musical mayhem at parties, they eventually became regular DJs at Naked Under Leather and London's Heavenly Sunday Social. They dubbed themselves the Dust Brothers in homage to the California production duo (Beastie Boys, Beck)...who eventually asked for the name back. By then, Tom and Ed—rechristened the Chemical Brothers—had come too far to be detained by mere matters of nomenclature.

Unable to find enough records boasting the flava they craved, the Brothers turned to making their own, starting with "Song to the Siren," a combustible combo of chunky beats, siren wails, and kidnapped samples. A slew of superlative follow-ups led to their 1995 debut *Exit Planet Dust*. Critics dubbed their sound big beat, and their success, both live and on the charts, paved the way for like-minded acts Fatboy Slim and Crystal Method.

In addition to their numerous studio efforts, the Chemical Brothers have unleashed two mix CDs, *Live at the Social, Volume One* and *Brother's Gonna Work It Out*. The year 1999 found the entire planet ensnared by their brilliant third album, *Surrender*, featuring collaborations with Oasis's Noel Gallagher, Bernard Sumner of New Order, and Mazzy Star songbird Hope Sandoval.

cultural ambassador and community leader, using music and his prominence as a force for social and political awareness and change and mixing different people harmoniously. Growing up in the '60s, he felt the influence of the civil rights movement and the Black Panthers. In later years he would often weave speeches by leaders like Martin Luther King Jr. and Malcolm X into his sets. But during the height of Bronx gang activity in the late '60s and early '70s, he'd been a member of the Black Spades, who offered a source of security and shelter amidst the surroundings of the impoverished neighborhood.

Bambaataa began DJing at house parties; interest in the art deepened when he discovered Kool Herc circa 1973. Increasingly disillusioned with gang life, he envisioned an alternative, a union forged to bolster a sense of community, both within the Bronx and beyond. Although he dallied with the Nation of Islam, he found their tenets too restrictive. Inspired by a British film about the Zulu of South Africa and their struggles to resist British colonialism, he adopted the name of the leader who'd fought to keep them free and dubbed his grassroots movement the Zulu Nation.

The Zulu Nation afforded crews a chance to battle for supremacy not with violence but via breaking, DJing, rapping, and painting, all under the sheltering umbrella of a loosely organized group. Although gang activity was waning in the Bronx by the mid-'70s, Bambaataa's prior involvement ensured him a built-in audience of followers early on, many of whom joined his nascent movement.

Almost a quarter of a century later, the organization is still going strong, with branches throughout the world. Forward thinking and openness to the opinions of all are central beliefs of the Zulu Nation philosophy. Although the group was an important force for black nationalism, they embrace people of all races, creeds, and categories. After all, hip-hop was born from multiculturalism: Caribbean-Americans (Kool DJ Herc), Puerto Ricans (Ruby Dee of the Fantastic Five, Futura 2000), and others were part of the genesis of hip-hop, too.

When hip-hop started it was a diverse experience. Hip-hop was made by the mixed people of Americas: Puerto Ricans, Africans, mixed Americans, a mixup of [ghetto] people. People who were living in the Bronx weren't only blacks. It was universal from the beginning.

—DJ Soul Slinger

For the first five or six years of its infancy, hip-hop music was disseminated largely via mix tapes from DJs' sets, played over boom boxes and car stereos. The culture spread to the other boroughs before slowly seeping into Manhattan, via cassettes overheard in taxicabs and art world curiosity concerning graffiti.

When the record industry finally took an interest in hip-hop, with '79–'80 releases like "Rapper's Delight" and Kurtis Blow's "The Breaks" (the second twelve-inch single to be certified for gold sales), it was the rhythmic delivery of the rappers they focused on. Although Grandmaster Flash & the Furious Five would push the medium further by integrating realistic social commentary into their 1982 hit "The Message," it was Flash's 1981 effort, "The Adventures of Grandmaster Flash on the Wheels of Steel," that truly inspired a new wave of DJs.

Created on three turntables in real time (that is, with no computers for smoothing out rough edges or overdubs for punching in corrections), "Wheels of Steel" represented the pinnacle of the DJ's craft at the time, incorporating the complete catalog of tricks. Without sacrificing musicality, Flash wove snippets of songs by Sugar Hill Gang, Blondie (who'd given him the nod on "Rapture" a year before), Queen, Chic, and the Sequence & Spoonie Gee together with "Apache," his own Furious Five cut "Birthday Party," a Flash Gordon radio play, and a comedy record into a dazzling collage that remained on beat for seven minutes.

"Wheels of Steel" was—and is and will always be—the most influential record I've ever heard. That was a time when records had one name and were made by an artist. All of the sudden, a DJ uses another person's records, and calls it his own...even though he hasn't actually recorded those pieces of music. That blew me away!

—Andy Smith

I was so young when I heard the first hip-hop records that I thought people scratched by taking a microphone and rubbing it on the floor. And I thought Grandmaster Flash made "Wheels of Steel" by cutting tapes together. I was ten years old—I didn't exactly know what *wheels of steel* meant. I started making these little mix tapes, cutting stuff together, and I made the scratching sound by rubbing this cheap children's microphone on the floor. It didn't really get the same sound, but I thought, *Maybe I'm not as good as them.*... But when I finally saw [hip-hop DJs] on TV and film, I went, "Now I get it!"

—Alec Empire

Like their underground disco peers, hip-hop DJs would make important musical contributions throughout the decade. Most notably, Afrika Bambaataa's 1982 single "Planet Rock" (which reflected his noted eclecticism by appropriating liberally from the German synthesizer quartet Kraftwerk), laid the framework for electro and much of the decade's progressive club music. Even though it was the rise of rap artists that garnered the most attention, the collective experience, the air of naïveté and enthusiasm of discovery that permeated the early hip-hop scene left an indelible impression on the shape of pop culture.

[Hip-hop] was this grass roots thing. I was lucky enough to pick up on it, to be there to see it in its infancy. Just hanging out with those people and following that style gave me something new to bring to the world when I made my own music.

—Kurtis Mantronik

4 The Young Person's Guide to Gear

I am not a tech-head. *Popular Mechanics* is a contradiction in terms, to my thinking. But unless you have magic powers and can play records by simply spinning them on your fingertip—in which case you have a zillion bookings already and are too busy to read this book—it behooves every DJ to have a working knowledge of the tools of the trade: turntables, needles, mixers. (We'll discuss CD players, digital audio tapes [DATs], and other recent developments later.) If you're serious about playing out, spend a few minutes doing research beyond the bare bones presented on the following pages. As my dad used to say, "If all else fails, read the manual." It's hard to maintain an air of cool around sound people or fellow DJs after pitching a hissy fit over the most mundane technical matter.

> If you use the best-quality equipment, it makes your life easier. If you've got a drum kit and it's cheap, the music you produce isn't going to sound as nice as the music a person with a professional drum kit makes.
>
> —Rob Swift

Turntables designed for DJs have special features: pitch control, quick stop/start, highly accurate revolution speeds. These facilitate ease of cuing, beat matching, and performing cuts and scratches. All turntables feature one of two types of motor: belt drive or direct drive. The former uses an oversize rubber band, attached to the motor, to spin the turntable platter (the surface on which the record sits). Belt drives have slower startup and recovery speeds. More important, cuing and scratching cause friction on the belt, which eventually wears smooth spots into the band, making the platter spin at uneven speeds. Ever run on an old treadmill at the gym and felt like it kept slipping under your feet? Same idea.

Direct-drive turntables feature a motor attached directly to the platter. These models feature faster stop/start functions, consistent revolutions, and improved torque (turning speed). The Technics SL 1200, the current industry standard for DJs, is direct drive.

Direct drives are also more durable. When I purchased my Technics, the vendor taped the warranty to the carton, then announced: "You'll never need this. These things are tanks." However, belt-drive turntables are markedly cheaper. If you're just learning your craft and money's tight, you might want to consider making the economical investment to start. Once you've gotten some chops on belt drives, using direct drives feels like a dream.

I'm from an era before those Technics 1200 turntables arrived, and even before pitch-control turntables. Using belt-drive turntables was pretty hard. They have a tendency to have a mind of their own.
—Juan Atkins

Direct drives were more expensive, but back then Technics hadn't perfected quartz lock and being stable. So if you had a direct-drive turntable and had to slow the record down by putting your finger on it, it would just lose pitch altogether. The belt drive would keep going; the belt would hold and slow down a little bit. So we had had belt drives back then.

—Jesse Saunders

MEET THE DJ

Juan Atkins

To kids growing up in this era of lucrative, high-profile club residencies, being a mobile DJ—spinning at parties, weddings, and so forth, for hire—might seem tacky, uncool. But Juan Atkins, the godfather of techno, would argue otherwise. "That type of experience definitely lends itself to traveling all over the world," says Juan. "When you're a mobile DJ, you're playing for different audiences, as opposed to your same crowd, every week."

As a teenager in Belleville, Michigan, near Detroit, Atkins became fascinated by early electronic pop: Gary Numan, Giorgio Moroder, George Clinton's P-funk projects. Influenced by the forward-thinking choices and mixing of radio DJs like Ken Collier and Charles Johnson, Juan and his friend Derrick May formed a DJs-for-hire crew, Deep Space Soundwork. With their mix of underground disco and European synth-pop, the pair worked very hard to keep discriminating audiences of affluent black teens dancing.

Prior to launching Deep Space, Atkins had begun making original music. In the early '80s he teamed with Rick Davis, a fellow community college student, as Cybotron. The duo's chilling android electro yielded seminal tracks, including "Clear" and "Techno City." The pair split in 1985, but Atkins moved on, launching the Metroplex label with his single "No UFOs," released under the name Model 500. Subsequent Metroplex releases, by Eddie Fowlkes, May, and Kevin Saunderson, introduced consumers to key techno innovators.

Juan's reputation was furthered by the late-'80s UK rave explosion. Roughly 5,000 dancers, mostly white, turned up for his first London gig—a far cry from the intimate dates Deep Space cut their teeth on. At the turn of the century, America is finally catching up.

Atkins continues to spin around the globe today and records extensively under several guises (Model 500, Infiniti, Channel One). His compilation *Juan Atkins Wax Trax! Mastermix Volume 1* provides a fantastic history lesson, spanning regional rarities (Sharevari's "A Number of Names"), local producers (Rob Hood, DJ Assault), and several of Atkins's personal best.

When I first started DJing, they didn't have 1200s. I had a set of B-1s, the belt-drive Technics. I had to be really agile and cautious on those. When I got on the 1200s, there was more flexibility and I was that much better.

—Prince Paul

I only worked one job on belt-drive turntables, and that was at Studio 54. I hated them so much that what I used to do was bring my own 1200s from home. I set great store by how I blend records, and belt-drive turntables are not helpful for executing slick, creative blending.

—Robbie Leslie

Assembling your own DJ setup isn't a cheap proposition. Just buying two turntables, a low-end mixer, and cartridges can quickly set you back well over $1,000. I drove three hours, across state lines, to avoid paying sales tax on my first set of decks. I felt like such an outlaw.

But also remember that hip-hop was born from an economy of means. It was cheaper for Kool Herc, Flash, and Bambaataa to turn it out with two turntables and a mixer than to assemble a slew of musicians. When Kemistry & Storm started out, they'd hook up various components from their individual stereos, plus parts of Goldie's, just to fashion one ramshackle system for late-night practicing. Don't let lack of access to top-of-the-line sound generators curtail your curiosity. Not everyone is born into a family like Rob Swift's....

I was lucky, because my dad is a DJ. He does parties and weddings. He always had two turntables, a mixer, and speakers in the house. He had great stuff, too, top quality. A lot of kids used to have to go over to friends' houses or deal with having one turntable, but I had everything. I just had to go buy the records.

—Rob Swift

MEET THE DJ

Studio K7

Kemistry & Storm

Although their aliases sound like superheroes', London's dynamic drum and bass duo Kemistry & Storm might be better described as partners in crime. "We became obsessed with the music together, and it went from there," says Kemistry. "We bought the records together, and the dream developed simultaneously. And because we'd learnt to DJ together, it was a logical progression to work together."

Having danced their way through the illegal UK party circuit in the late '80s, the pair eventually landed at Fabio and Grooverider's legendary Rage night, practically ground zero for the breakbeat hardcore/jungle/drum and bass scene. Soon they'd dragged their graffiti artist buddy Goldie down, and he was hooked as well.

The trio learned their craft as a team, connecting various parts from their individual stereos into one big system. "We'd all go out, then come back, and say, 'Let's pretend to be DJs,'" remembers Storm. "But all we could do was play tracks and rewind 'em. We couldn't do anything else. We'd do that for hours, have our own little raves in the bedroom."

In 1991, the threesome took to the airwaves on pirate station Touchstone FM, with Goldie rapping over the women's beats. When he launched his Metalheadz label in 1994, they came along; as his career as a recording artist ascended, Kemistry & Storm took up the slack, assuming an increasing number of duties, until their own DJ bookings became so prolific that they passed on the reins, too.

With their position at the epicenter of drum and bass affording them access to the hottest tracks, Kemistry & Storm remain dedicated to championing a variety of the highest-quality cuts. "We're purists about drum and bass—we don't really listen to any other kind of music—but we love every part of it," says Storm. For a sample, check out their 1999 installment of the STUD!O K7 *DJ Kicks* series.

Tragically, Kemi Olusanya, alias DJ Kemistry, died in a car accident early on the morning of Sunday, April 25, 1999. She and Storm were returning from an engagement in Southampton, ninety minutes southeast of London, when their car struck a loose divider in the middle of the road. She was the lone fatality.

You cannot be a DJ and not have your own turntables and a mixer.

—DJ Soul Slinger

Because I was hungry at the time, I learned to make do with what I had. Putting those wires together and using crappy equipment gave me an understanding early on. I didn't have money to go out and get good equipment. But because I accomplished what I did with that junk, that showed me that I should be in music.

—Kurtis Mantronik

I had a Lafayette turntable, from one of those cheap phonographs. Plus I had a component set that my family had; I took the old one that nobody wanted, fixed it, and pieced it together. I was into the whole electronics thing as well. So I had two turntables. And I hooked [the other turntable] up through an auxiliary and used the balance, left and right, as a mixer. I put the sound out in mono, so it came out of the same speaker, as opposed to left and right. I had no cue. That was my first setup, and that balance knob got really worn out and wobbly after a while.

—Prince Paul

There was a time before mixing came in when you had one turntable on the phono line and one on the auxiliary line [on a receiver]. You'd have to switch between the phono and auxiliary lines to get something like a segue. There was no cuing. You'd cue by looking at the record. You know how sometimes you can hear through the needle on top [of the vinyl]? You'd try to listen to that. The guy [who] could get the record on and still get the intro and leave the least amount of space in between each record was the top guy.

—Juan Atkins

MEET THE DJ

Rob Swift of the X-ecutioners

Growing up in Jackson Heights, Queens, in the '70s and '80s, Rob Swift fell in love with rap. Back then, the DJ was at the heart of the action. So as far as he and his fellow X-ecutioners are concerned, hip-hop's current penchant for rhyming over well-known oldies constitutes the lowest form of making tracks. Instead, Swift (who is also a contributing editor to Rap Pages) dedicates himself wholeheartedly to promoting the turntable as a distinct instrument.

Like many of his fellow turntablists, Grandmixer D.ST's scratching on Herbie Hancock's 1983 MTV smash "Rockit" prompted Swift's revelation. "Before that, my view towards the art was really limited, as far as what you could do with the turntable and scratching." Suddenly a new dimension, far beyond rudimentary juggling of beats and phrases, opened up.

Swift emulated the mastery of men he admired: Doctor Butcher, Cash Money, Stevie D and D.ST. Fortunately, his father was a mobile jock, so access to equipment wasn't an obstacle. As he matured, so did the art form, culminating in the current climate, when DJs have returned to the foreground.

In 1989, a group of New York battle DJs joined forces as the X-Men to challenge another crew, the Supermen. Renamed the X-ecutioners today, the quartet—Swift, Roc Raida, Total Eclipse, and Mista Sinista—has helped transform the intricate scratches and tricks of the competition circuit into a unique medium of expression. The group's 1997 debut *X-pressions* minimized rhyming to emphasize juxtapositions of ear-catching snippets, thus making the turntable the nucleus of each track.

Swift's solo album *The Ablist* upped the ante, showcasing his skills as a producer and MC, too, in a set that owed as much to improvisational jazz as rap. "I made a conscious effort to show how effectively the turntable can be used within a studio environment to compose and perform different songs." He succeeded, hopefully providing a jumping-off point for a new generation primed to take the decks to the next level.

Recently, Vestax—a manufacturer best known for its mixers—raised the bar slightly by introducing new-model turntables with additional gizmos aimed at DJs, particularly turntablists. The Vestax PDX-a2 MKII features a vertical position design (so the tone arm doesn't get in the way when you're scratching), two stop/start buttons (one on each side of the platter, eliminating a spot for a 45 adaptor), and a wider range of pitch control. But not everyone waits around for the big boys to fashion a product that meets his or her unique needs.

> One of my turntables goes backward. It has a switch and it'll play backward. This guy from England, he comes to town every couple of months, and he'll modify turntables for people. I'd seen them at parties, so I got one of mine done.
>
> —Heather Heart

Regardless of your turntable type, slipmats are essential for every DJ. These little devils allow the DJ to control his or her vinyl while the platter beneath spins freely at full speed. The most popular type is just a thin circular sheet of felt. You can purchase them in a variety of decorator patterns from any good record store, or simply fashion a couple out of felt from a fabric or craft shop. Make certain that they're not too thick and that the spindle hole is loose if you want to use them smoothly.

Alternately, just snip a couple out of the plastic sleeves inside a record jacket. This is a great trick in a pinch if you show up at a gig to find decks with no slipmats. Original hip-hop DJs sometimes used pieces of cardboard, or two 45s stacked on top of each other. Today, some pros, like Shortkut from Invisbl Skratch Piklz, swear by putting plastic between your regular slipmat and the platter: "It's like having oil right under your record." (Eeeeew!) On a related note, purportedly some turntablists and scratch DJs literally apply furniture polish directly to the platter.

When we first got our decks, we mixed with the rubber mats that come with the Technics on for two weeks, and thought, *Oh my God, the decks are really stiff . . . I hope we're going to get the hang of this.* And then our friend who DJs came around and said, "Something's wrong here. You've still got the rubber mats on!"

—Storm (Kemistry & Storm)

I never really knew how slipmats actually worked. It wasn't until the first time I put my hand on a record and froze it that I realized "This thing is traveling at full speed."

—Peter Calandra

The most important parts of any turntable are the cartridge and the stylus. The stylus tracks the groove on a record, gliding over microscopic bumps and crevices. In turn, the cartridge translates these movements into electronic signals, which are amplified into sound. There are two types of styluses, named for their different needle shapes: spherical and elliptical. Most DJs argue the former track better and wear less on records.

That last factor is a key concern. The antiskating, tone arm counterweight, and height adjustment settings on a turntable affect how much pressure the needle places on the record when tracking it. But the stylus is ultimately the only thing rubbing up against your precious vinyl. Cheap or worn-out styluses can accelerate the accumulation of cue burns, resulting in excessive static...often on your favorite jams! Take time to find the stylus that works best for you. Ortofon, Stanton, and Shure manufacture the most popular models, but they don't have a monopoly by any means.

I prefer Ortofon styluses because they're lighter. I find Stantons a bit heavy, and they really gouge in, but a lot of people use Stantons. It all depends on how heavy you are with your hands and how you set your decks up. You need to try a few different ones in the shop.

—Andy Smith

69

MEET THE DJ

Heather Heart

Heather Heart's name may not register on the radar of Middle America like the Prodigy or the Chemical Brothers, but if it wasn't for this Brooklyn native and her friends Frankie Bones and Adam X, the U.S. rave scene would be radically different.

"I've been a big record collector, since I was eleven or twelve," enthuses Heart. But when she and her pals discovered techno, they found their calling. Their STORMrave events started out small but soon blossomed. "Back in '91, we were just doing our own parties, for ten or twenty people. I never said, 'I want to be a DJ.' I just fell into it."

Heather also published the influential *Under One Sky* from 1991–94. "I started the fanzine because more people were getting into the music, but they didn't know where it was coming from. I wanted to push the DJs and producers and educate people [who] were coming into the scene."

Heart's discography includes contributions to the 1995 double-pack twelve-inch "A Track Is a Track Is a Track" and her 1994 collaboration with Adam X, "Brooklyn to the Core." Her 1998 mix tape *Eastbound Underground 1* offers a taste of her "smooth purist techno" recorded live. As the title of her EP *Analogistic Warrior* implies, Heart adamantly champions old analog equipment (she's featured in the documentary *Better Living through Circuitry* with her vintage gear).

When she's not playing parties or maintaining **www.underonesky.net**, Heather continues promoting the scene at a grassroots level as co-owner of Sonic Groove, a Manhattan-based record store and label. "Now we're pressing labels and distributing records. It's important that companies other than the big guys are pushing underground music. If we can start to press for a label that was struggling to sell two hundred records and help them sell one thousand, that's a good thing."

Some needles are worse than others, and they really fuck your records up. I have records from back when I didn't know that I'll play now, and all you hear is static. Now I use Shure needles; they're the best. They don't really burn shit out as much. You just learn as you go along.

—Rob Swift

I'm not super particular about my needles. I want a good quality needle. So I don't want any crap, but I don't go, "I must have Trackmaster Pros," or anything like that.

—Richie Hawtin (Plastikman)

Larry Levan used to rhapsodize about outfitting his multiple turntables with different grades of cartridges so as the night progressed he could upgrade the quality of the styluses and continue refining the sound of the music he played.

Some DJs bring their own needles to gigs; others don't. It's a matter of personal choice. If you carry your own, you know exactly how good the styluses touching your records will be. Many clubs and parties know they're paying a tidy sum to book a DJ and already have top-notch cartridges on hand. Others assume that the DJ will be carrying their own and thus merely have something run-of-the-mill—or worse yet, nothing at all—installed.

I remember showing up for one of my first lounge dates to discover the cartridges for both decks were missing and having to borrow some from the DJ in the club's main room. (He subsequently bequeathed his spares to me, thus saving me future embarrassment till I'd purchased my own—I didn't have turntables yet.) I think that hoping that styluses will be already installed and will always be of good quality is as sensible as traveling without a toothbrush and just borrowing your host's wherever you stay. Eventually, you're going to be sorry.

I used to bring my own needles everywhere. But I can't say no, [so] everyone else would be using them. And I've had so many needles break on me because other people were using them. For that reason alone, it became a hassle. I got tired of having to buy new needles every time I came home.

—DJ Tron

I've been to a lot of gigs where I've said to myself, *I'm going to start carrying my own needles around.* But when you start carrying your own needles around, then there's something else that goes wrong. That's almost predicting catastrophe before it happens . . . . Plus that's just an extra thing you've got to carry around. Like now—I forgot my damn headphones in Detroit. I had to borrow a pair of headphones.

—Juan Atkins

Every DJ I know (including all the ones interviewed for this book) brings his or her own headphones. Think of them as a security blanket—they fit your head already. Besides, you don't want somebody else's stale sweat in your ears, do you? If you've got room in your bag, a record cleaner is a good idea, too. Especially if you're aiming to play on the rave circuit at parties held in big, desolate warehouses and abandoned airports.

I do bring my own headphones, just because I'm comfortable with them. They're so worn and ragged that they just fit my ear.

—DJ Tron

I bring my own headphones; I don't bring my own needles. And I bring a record cleaner because playing in these places, my records get really dusty.

—Heather Heart

The range of mixers available for DJs runs the gamut, from rinky-dink ones like Peanut Butter Wolf's first from Radio Shack to models that rival the behemoths found in recording studios. Most importantly, you want a smooth, clean cross-fader (no static!). In a perfect world, your mixer will have EQ knobs for each line, so you can control the various sonic frequencies, which facilitates better-integrated mixes and allows you to tweak a record's dynamics, rendering your musical materials more malleable.

> One thing I learned about from Jeff Mills and Derrick May and those guys was EQ, cranking up the midrange and taking out the bass. That was really a Detroit phenomenon. I know in Chicago and New York they were taking out bass and stuff like that, but in Detroit it was really accentuated. Bringing things down to where you could hardly hear them, going down to nearly silence, and then slowly bringing them up. It was always about modifying the records as much as possible. I can remember, five or six years ago, when it wasn't even common in clubs to have EQs on the mixing board. Sound engineers and clubs didn't want the DJ playing with it. If I get to a club now and there's no EQ, I'll play, but it's a handicap. People expect a certain thing from me, or at least expect the unexpected. How can I do that when I'm presented with something with a set number of rules?
>
> —Richie Hawtin (Plastikman)

More advanced mixers feature sampling capability, effects buttons, and so on, but you don't really need to worry about that stuff until you kick ass on the wheels of steel. When you've got all those bells and whistles at your disposal, getting carried away is easy. You can put all the creamy frosting in the world on a brick, but that doesn't make it a cupcake.

Ultimately, every time you set foot outside your door to spin, you're taking chances. Like rock bands, major DJs have equipment

MEET THE DJ

Richie Hawtin (alias Plastikman)

Like many prominent DJs, Richie Hawtin—aka Plastikman—entered the life as a consequence of his record collection. The story's twist is that Richie wasn't the one who determined he should share his vast knowledge of electronic music publicly; his buddies made the decision.

"My friends and I just wanted to hear the music," he explains. In nearby Detroit, there were radio programs featuring such fare by the mid-'80s. But across the border, in Hawtin's hometown of Windsor, Ontario, Canada, options were limited. So Richie's friends asked a local youth club for a shot at throwing a weekly party, and since Richie had the best music (encompassing everything from Skinny Puppy to his father's Kraftwerk and Tangerine Dream LPs), he became the DJ.

After this six-month amateur stint, Richie retreated to the family basement to practice in solitude. The next time he emerged, it was to accept a warm-up slot at the legendary Detroit club Shelter. "Coming in and playing a couple [of] records for free turned into playing at the start and the end, to getting twenty bucks, then fifty..." remembers Richie. Coming up through the ranks during Detroit's golden age, Richie witnessed and learned from the early techno masters: Kevin Saunderson, Derrick May, Juan Atkins, Jeff Mills.

Initially, Richie's signature style as both a DJ and recording artist bore distinct markings of Motor City minimalism, taking spartan tracks and then magnifying and manipulating them via a barrage of effects. His first two Plastikman albums (he records under several other monikers, most notably F.U.S.E.), 1993's *Sheet One* and 1994's *Musik* were tweaked-out acid masterpieces, electrifying hot wires to the listener's head.

For the next four years, Hawtin kept a lower profile, concentrating on more experimental offerings and DJ commitments, before resurfacing in 1998. His most recent Plastikman full-lengths, *Consumed* and *Artifakts [BC]*, feature a stripped-down, slower sound. In contrast, his integrated shows—extended affairs of invigorating ebb and flow—continue to blur distinctions between DJ and live performer further. For a sample, check out his mix CD *Decks, EFx, & 909.*

riders that spell out what they expect to find when they arrive. But even that's not a guarantee. Sometimes it's best to just expect the unexpected. And always try to make friends with whoever is in charge of the sound—they can either be your fiercest ally or completely undermine your set.

I'm not strict about technical details. I don't put that information in my riders. If people are going to hire a world-class DJ, I'm going to give them the benefit of the doubt that they're going to have the best equipment they can get...or at least something functional.

—Juan Atkins

The worst thing by far—and I don't care about hotels or transport or waiting in the airport—is when I don't have a cross-fader. And although my contract specifies there should be one, I do get to gigs and there's no cross-fader. That's ridiculous. You're stopping me from doing half of what you're paying me for. And promoters are like, "Oh, sorry...can you not manage without?"

—Andy Smith

In America, it's still a rock and roll mentality at a lot of the clubs, although it's getting better. In Europe even the rock and roll companies have now done so much stuff with electronic music that they know how to tweak the sounds. There's a certain art form to having the right soundman to even EQ electronic music, making it sound right. It goes way beyond just the DJ.

—Richie Hawtin (Plastikman)

I still don't have my own tech [roadie]. I do all the setup myself. I can't trust anybody else. I'll go up there in front of ten thousand people with the road crew, wave to the kids, and check my equipment to make sure it's all in good shape.

—DJ Lethal

I've lost count of the number of times I've seen a club where hundreds of thousands were spent on the lights but the sound system was a heap of shit. Alternately, you'd be at a rock venue where the road crews really hate DJs and don't know how to set up the decks.

—Mixmaster Morris

I heard a very funny story from John Stapleton, who does the *Dope on Plastic* compilations. He was DJing with Crash Slaughter, who's a hip-hop DJ from Scotland, playing this really posh club in France. They wanted four turntables set up so John could play the tunes and Crash could scratch on top. They went into the club, and they worked out that one pair of decks—the ones John was to use—were okay. But the other two weren't working. They went to the sound engineer and said, "These two decks are okay, but the other ones aren't." He said, "Okay," and took the phono plugs out of the [decks] that were working and plugged them into the other two, and said, "There you go!" And he was the chief engineer in this club!

—Andy Smith

5 Looking for the Perfect Beat

A DJ's music collection is his or her most important resource. Without sounds to share, all the mad skills, intuitive understanding of crowd dynamics, and well-oiled equipment won't do you much good. Obviously, the likelihood that every slab of wax a DJ owns is eligible for inclusion in a set is slim, but the possibility is always there. And regardless, every piece of music a DJ has ever listened to informs his or her sensibility.

For a lot of DJs, a deep love for music, instilled by family members, underscored the medium's powerful emotional pull from a very early age.

My dad died when I was three and left me his collection of old jazz and blues records. I've been building on that ever since. I can just imagine my dad. He was a connoisseur, and very picky. He wasn't into density. He had a very solid jazz collection, but he didn't go out and buy everything.

—DJ Spooky

I started DJing with my mom's records. She bought the first two hundred records, and then the billions of things I began collecting came along. Once I became a DJ, I started digging in my aunt's records, going over to people's houses, looking through their collections.

—Afrika Bambaataa

I always had the biggest record collection of all my friends, because my sister was a music freak. She was into Elvis. And my parents were both total pop music fanatics. They were into Sinatra. We always had a charge account at the record store.

—Anita Sarko

My whole family collected records: my brothers, sisters. My father had a huge jazz collection. At least I thought it was huge at the time. I'd blow him out by comparison about a million times over now. My mom had a stack of records. Our whole family life was centered around the record player in the living room.

—Prince Paul

My uncle's always been a big record collector. Then, when I was young, he got into reel-to-reel tapes and wanted space in his house. He didn't want records anymore. He put everything on to reel-to-reel and said to me, "Come and take the records." I took them all. That's what made me get into funk, Parliament and the whole Dr. Funkenstein thing.

—Jumping Jack Frost

Emerging music fanatics quickly tire of riffling through their folks' records. You want your own tunes, albums and singles that say something to—and about—you and your developing personality. A cursory glance through the youthful stacks of certain established DJs might reveal an even greater range of taste than their current station implies.

When I was really young I had a huge record collection. I was always aware of club music. I had all the old West End and Prelude releases, by D-Train and Sharon Redd. I was probably the only kid in school who actually knew of that music. Everybody else was into rock. But I was still into disco.

—Andy Smith

Other than punk rock records, I had zero to ten techno records when I started DJing. Before that, I'd ask the DJ, "What is that?" if I heard something I liked at a club. Lords of Acid's "I Sit on Acid" still sticks in my head. And "French Kiss" by Lil' Louis was so much fun. I'd take a record home and listen to it for hours.

—DJ Tron

In certain instances, it was a record collection that dictated a nascent DJ's initial foray into the field. How different my life might have been had I never bought that Shirley Bassey version of "Copacabana."

When the father, Kool DJ Herc, came out with the hip-hop sound, I said, "Wait, I've got those records, and then some." I was playing crazy stuff at my parties and got dubbed the Master of Records. A lot of the beats in hip-hop come from Zulu Nation standards.

—Afrika Bambaataa

I started DJing because I loved music initially. I was collecting records long before I DJed. But Bambaataa's record collection was incredible. He'd spin everything. He had records that to this day, when I'll be listening to old tapes, I don't know what it is he's playing.

—Prince Paul

MEET THE DJ

Phyllis Galembo

DJ Spooky

"I think most people are so conditioned by the dance music aesthetic that there has to be four to the beat," said Paul D. Miller—alias DJ Spooky, That Subliminal Kid—with a sigh in 1998. "I look at music more as a vehicle for aesthetic inspiration." Spooky's sets are just as likely to incorporate outrè jazz master Sun Ra or electronic innovator Luciano Berio as Wu-Tang Clan.

Throughout the '90s, Miller's writing, music, and visual art has both intrigued fans and enraged detractors. "All my artwork is an extension of my writing, and my writing deals with the immersion of the human consciousness into the extended network of electronic media." Human beings have become inextricable from the matrix of media we originally created. DJ Spooky's various creations dive headfirst into that twenty-first-century sea of possibilities.

Miller was raised in Washington, D.C., surrounded by cultural activity and political consciousness. In the D.C. scene, outsider music wasn't segregated on bills. Hearing a hardcore punk band, a go-go group, and a reggae crew at the same show didn't shock. He spent summers in Jamaica and traveled to Africa.

"I'd always looked to New York in the early '80s as my model," says Spooky of his aesthetic, referring to the abstract mentality embodied at downtown clubs. In college, his unorthodox radio show *Dr. Seuss's Eclectic Jungle* orchestrated assorted sources into barely contained chaos. "But when I got to New York, I realized, 'Jesus Christ, everybody is completely in a musical box!'" Frustrated with the restrictive attitudes he encountered, Miller threw his own parties instead.

Today, DJ Spooky's list of accomplishments is as variegated as his mix tapes. His earlier recordings, *The Necropolis Dialogic Project* and *Songs of a Dead Dreamer*, distilled the urban energy of the Information Age into baffling soundscapes; the recent Riddim Warfare translated similar concepts into more accessible contexts. If any individual best represents the DJ as a filter for organizing information and history to create new connections between cultures and ideas, Spooky is the number-one contender.

One of the reasons that I ended up being a DJ was I came to terms with the fact that these records that were being pressed as limited edition extended versions weren't going to be in circulation forever. Before you know it, my record collection started building. Within the first five years of collecting, I must have had about three-thousand twelve-inch singles.

—Peter Calandra

I started buying records in about '76, whenever the first punk records started coming out. Punk music was difficult to find at that point, and only weirdo specialist shops dealt in it. So you'd go there, and they're full of weirdo strange bobs who are into all sorts of other music.

—Jonathan More (Coldcut)

Jon had an incredible amount of music, with what we call a left-foot approach to it. He was into African and weird New York productions, everything up to [minimalist composer] Steve Reich. At the time, most other DJs—and there weren't many around in 1983–'84—were pretty well focused on their specific style of music, but Jon's scope was always wider.

—Matt Black (Coldcut)

In the early days, I tried to buy two of everything, so I could collect one and mess one up. But it cost me a fortune, so I gave it up.

—Paul Oakenfold

How often, and where and for what a DJ goes music shopping ultimately boils down to an extensive menu of individual concerns. What do you like to play? How often are you working? How much time are you willing to devote to the hunt? How much money do you have? Certain DJs place supreme importance on always being ahead of the pack with fresh titles.

If you're making mix tapes once a month, you should keep up with records and have all the new ones, because people want to hear new stuff.

—Rob Swift

You have to go to the shops at least once a week, to be abreast of the new things.

—Juan Atkins

It's very important to be on top of what you're doing. I make the time to track down tunes that nobody else has got: ringing various DJs to get DATs, ringing record companies to get acetates; going to specialist's stores; being a member of four record pools in New York; being in touch with European record companies.

—Paul Oakenfold

Of course, if you're not world famous (yet), magazine reviews, recommendations from peers and friends, and loyalty to names with proven track records can all provide clues for finding records that may float your boat...and your crowds'.

I follow the strength of labels and producers. There are a few labels, especially in what we do, that you can pretty much trust unconditionally. I've not bought a record that I regretted for a couple of years now.

—Scott Hendy (Purple Penguin)

Ultimately, the best judge of whether a record is right for you is your ears. Listening stations in stores are a fantastic but fairly recent development in customer service. If the opportunity is available to preview the music, take the extra time to do so—bearing in mind there are probably other customers waiting behind you. Skip over listening and you inevitably wind up with a higher percentage of new records you're less likely to cherish.

> Now everybody has turntable stations. But when I first started shopping, you had to have the guy behind the counter play them for you. And when you're five-foot-three and these big DJs are in front of you, on a raised platform that [you] can't even reach up to, that's intimidating.
>
> —Emily Ng

You can learn plenty about someone's interests from the contents of his or her wallet. Some people carry photos of the spouse and kids; most single young men I know pack condoms. But yours truly? Moist towelettes. Because the grime on my hands after flipping through most used-record bins is enough to turn Pigpen into a Howard Hughes neat freak. Not that I'm complaining. Two of the finest vintage techno jams in my crates—Eddie "Flashin" Fowlkes's "Goodbye Kiss" and "R-9" by Juan Atkins's Cybotron—were both obtained for pennies in thrift stores.

Some DJs relentlessly comb used-record stores and secondhand vendors looking for rare grooves rendered seminal by their predecessors. If you're poor or just starting out, used vinyl provides an excellent way to expand your collection. But most of us simply suffer from an insatiable need for a constant influx of music.

> There's a chronic Ninja addiction to vinyl, which I've managed to wean myself off slightly. But I can't speak for our more seriously addicted brothers.
>
> —Matt Black (Coldcut)

> I still do charity shops and car boot sales. I had a wicked find the other day, some very obscure electronic records. A collection of weird electronics from Czechoslovakia, John Cage's *Fontana Mix* in mint condition, John Cage's *Prepared Pianos*, never been played. All for three quid each!
>
> —Jonathan More (Coldcut)

MEET THE DJ

Coldcut

What do you think of when someone says "coldcut"? Salami...or the most prescient duo of artist-innovators to emerge from the British dance scene? The creations of Coldcut may be composed almost exclusively from chopped-up beats and pieces, but their fortifying fare is all meat, no filler.

Ex-art instructor Jonathan More and computer programmer Matt Black hooked up in the mid-'80s, bonding over their mutual love for hip-hop pioneers like Double Dee & Steinski ("Lesson 1"). Matt excelled at the technical side of the craft, whereas Jon possessed an incredibly eclectic record collection, from African tribal recordings to the minimalism of Steve Reich.

The pair started spinning at clubs like Shoom, then garnered acclaim for their *Solid State* radio show on KISS-FM (seek out their dizzying *70 Minutes of Madness* contribution to the *Journeys by DJ* series). Their first single, 1987's "Say Kids (What Time Is It?)" was a cut-and-paste masterpiece, kicking off a wave of similar hits by M/A/R/R/S, Bomb the Bass, and S'Express. Soon after, their radical overhaul of Eric B. & Rakim's "Paid in Full" redefined what constituted a remix.

Disillusioned with the mainstream music business, the duo launched their Ninjatune label shortly after releasing their second album, *Philosophy*, in late '93. With a roster of open-minded DJs and musicians—including DJ Food, Funki Porcini, Amon Tobin, and Mixmaster Morris—Ninjatune is a name discerning consumers trust. Meanwhile, their Stealth night was named club of the year by several UK style bibles.

Today Coldcut continues expanding the boundaries of DJ culture. *Let Us Replay* included a CD-ROM of their V-Jamm software, an integral element of their live performances, which allows the user to loop, scratch, and chop up audiovisual samples. Coldcut recognizes that the days when a DJ's tools were simply two turntables, a mixer, and a stack of wax have long since passed. For these "data jockeys," all sounds and images are raw materials to be reconfigured in the name of art, technology, and a top night out.

The last time I went to Japan, I was out there with a few guys. And everyone was saying, "I've got to go and look for all this new musical equipment, new technology." But where's Frost? In the secondhand record shops, digging through the crates, wondering if there's anything I've missed.

—Jumping Jack Frost

You can find good records anywhere, even places that are well known. Because of the fact that they are well known, people come and sell their records to them all the time, too. It's just a matter of going frequently.

—Peanut Butter Wolf

I've got my own mobile record deck, but it broke. So Andy Smith lent me this Fisher-Price to come out with on this U.S. trip, and it's just wonderful.

—Scott Hendy (Purple Penguin)

That takes a bit of the fun out of it, though, sitting in the shop and discarding stuff.

—Ben Dubuisson (Purple Penuin)

But at least then you don't have to do the car boot sale and flog 'em.

—Scott Hendy

I have a friend who goes to estates all the time, when somebody passes away. He gets whole collections that way. That's his secret. Put that in the book.

—Peanut Butter Wolf

If you're a producer or DJ with an ear for sampling and a fascination for the way dance music recycles materials and ideas, used records can be an even greater resource.

First you'd hear hip-hop tunes that sampled all these old James Brown records. But then you'd you hear the original and go, "Wow!" Remember the first time you heard "Funky Drummer?" What a time that was! Then you realize there's loads of this music, and it's really good! So when I started hearing hip-hop, I started collecting all the '70s stuff it sampled as well.

—Andy Smith

When I first started, I was buying all the James Brown and Stanley Turentine records, all the jazz stuff, the Headhunters and the Meters. I got done with the classics pretty fast. Those records were already pretty played out back in '89. So I started getting weird, bugged-out records.

—DJ Lethal

Various records I've bought, I'm not going to play them out. They're just for samples. I don't know why people go out and pay big money for a sample record. What's the point in that? There's something you can take and turn around on every record. Why spend one hundred fifty dollars?

—Scott Hendy (Purple Penguin)

Over time, most DJs find their tastes changing and becoming more refined. They get much more particular about what they purchase. With the continued proliferation of dance music across the board, there are certainly more releases to choose from in any given week. And yet, if your ears are especially seasoned, a lot of them don't seem so terribly new.

MEET THE DJ

Gabby Lang

DJ Emily

Given her background, it's not shocking that Emily Ng—also known as DJ Emily—has established a healthy career working in music. But what might surprise her old classmates from New York's LaGuardia High School of Music and Arts ("The *Fame* school," she says with a chuckle) is her line of work; the girl they knew as a so-so flute player has grown up to be a hotly touted international house DJ.

Even before she'd completed her classical course of studies, Emily was a club kid, seduced by the sounds of Junior Vasquez and Frankie Knuckles. "I just loved that music, and I wanted to have it," she reveals. Since bootleg tapes purchased on the streets couldn't guarantee consistent quality of programming, Ng started rounding up all her personal favorites on vinyl. Soon she'd acquired two turntables and started compiling her own mixes.

Her career took a quantum leap forward when friends doing promotion for Peter Gatien's now-defunct Club USA offered her a plum spot in the Thierry Mugler Room, even though she was virtually unknown...but not for long. "That was my first gig, and I was hooked after that." She spent the months that followed honing her craft, working at a couple of labels, and slowly making inroads.

Since then, her commitments have snowballed. In 1997, Emily signed on as the Friday-night mix-show DJ for New York dance radio outpost WKTU. The following year, she became the host of the weekly internet broadcast *Global House* (on the Pseudo network), championing underground dance music before an ever-widening international audience. Her deep, hard, and—sadly—unreleased version of Grace Jones's "Cradle to Grave" attracted additional industry attention and led to gigs remixing Kim English ("Tomorrow") and Delirium ("Duende").

In the physical world circa 1999, DJ Emily can be found spinning at such venues as New York's Life and Ottawa's Industry; she also has a residency at D! in Lausanne, Switzerland. Her own debut EP, *The Disco Bandit*, was released on Deep Dish's Yoshitoshi label, and her vocals are featured on Todd Terry's single "Blackout."

I don't listen to dance music anymore. Every time I listen to a record, all I hear is "Love Is the Message," or variations on that. So I'd rather just go put on "Love Is the Message."

—Steve D'Acquisto

Eight or ten years ago, there was a smaller amount of records to listen to every week. And the percentage of quality releases was higher. It was very easy to go into a store and pick up a record and go, "Wow! I've never heard anything like that before in my life!" There were advances being made every week. Now we've defined what we're doing; ten years ago, it was intangible. There are still probably eight records that, in my opinion, are good [every week] now, but I'd probably have to go through twenty or thirty others.

—Richie Hawtin (Plastikman)

And what's with all the funny genre names? Do they really help us distinguish types of music or do they just make underpaid record-store clerks with inferiority complexes feel better about their jobs?

I used to hear people say, "Oh, the latest blah-blah-blah release, it's got a real such-and-such feel...." When I look back on it now, I realize those guys didn't know what the hell they were talking about! There are no definitive genres in house music. People just try to break it down into little subsections just for the sake of communicating, but they didn't know.

—Emily Ng

Terms like *techno, house,* and so on just make me laugh, because you can very well have several of them at the same time: a heavy metal–go-go–techno record.

Matt Black (Coldcut)

Record collections have a way of expanding to fill any space available. This is particularly dangerous if you're fond of perusing secondhand bins ("Oh, it's only a dollar—I can't pass it up....") and/or receiving a lot of promos. Vinyl obtained for a song still takes up just as much space as expensive import titles. This is a basic rule of physics all DJs might want to consider getting tattooed on a highly noticeable part of their body.

I have about seventy thousand LPs and thirty thousand 45s. I'm at the point where I don't buy anything I've ever seen or heard or cared about knowing about. I have every standard soul, R&B, or funk record from '60 on.

—DJ Lethal

I probably have about thirty-something thousand records.

—DJ Spooky

I just came out with an album called "My Vinyl Weighs a Ton." Basically each record weighs half a pound, so four thousand records would be two thousand pounds, one ton. I came up with the name just carrying crates around. I was moving into a new house and had to carry my records up two flights of stairs. My girlfriend's dad said, "You must have a ton of records," and calculated it out. I'd say I have well over a ton.

—Peanut Butter Wolf

I've got one hundred seventy-five feet of records. That's if you took down all my shelves. But I've got loads in boxes on the floor. I thought seven or eight thousand, but maybe more.

—Jonathan More (Coldcut)

Jon's just bought a house, so he's got his record space there,

MEET THE DJ

Purple Penguin

"When we DJ, we like to mix it all up and have a good time, a bit of a laugh," says Ben Dubuisson, one half of Purple Penguin. "We might drop in the theme tune from some old TV show, like *The A-Team*, as an introduction to some beats." Vintage jazz, funk, reggae, and hip-hop figure heavily into their mix, too.

The pair's playful programming seems downright ebullient considering their hometown—Bristol, a British city with rainfall that rivals Seattle's. Then factor in the dour face painted on this northern town by brooding exports like Massive Attack, Portishead, and Tricky. "We don't take ourselves too seriously," admits Ben. "A lot of people do. But that's a stance they take for effect a lot of the time."

Dubuisson and partner Scott Hendy had each worked extensively as live musicians and DJs before meeting in 1994 at one of the influential Cup of Tea club nights. "We were already doing very similar things," says Scott. "It was just a matter of time before we joined forces." Ben had an ear for beat matching and mixing, whereas Scott excelled at scratching; both shared a deep love for down-tempo tracks, hip-hop, and odd obscurities.

A similar sensibility—clipped beats anchoring jazzy cadences—underscores the team's sublime albums *De-Tuned* and *Question*. The former title helped establish the Cup of Tea record label's reputation as top-notch merchants of chill beats; the latter bristles with greater stylistic diversity and range of musical colors.

With their star slowly on the rise, 1998 saw Purple Penguin invited to play live at select jazz festivals, and both members have ongoing side projects. Ben's copious free time finds him at his record store (also named Purple Penguin), which stocks the bread and butter for many of Bristol's finest: hip-hop, drum and bass, breaks and beats, and Mo' Wax—style grooves. Hendy is also responsible for the percolating compilation *Turbo Beats*.

even though it's many, many meters. He's managed to consign the family to a couple of small rooms.

—Matt Black (Coldcut)

I have so many records that I don't know what to do with them. They're everywhere. I have about fifty or sixty crates' worth, and I only have forty actual crates, so the rest of them are on the floor. I've got to get some sort of shelf system. It's getting really bad. I'm going to have to start tunneling through my apartment!

—Heather Heart

A sprawling record collection can pose certain obstacles if you're trying to accommodate a lover, family, or pet into your crowded home. But getting rid of records feels like being forced to pick sad-eyed Dickensian urchins out of a lineup at an overpopulated orphanage at Christmas and proclaim, "You, you, and you...out in the snow you go!" Fortunately, if the experiences of some of the more polished pros interviewed are any indication, there may be hope for saps like me in sight. "Why carry around twenty thousand pieces of vinyl when all this house music is summed up in two hundred pieces of vinyl [and] the rest is derivative, just a variation?" New York producer Daniel Wang argued a few years ago.

I'm looking at my record shelves right now, which—after several disastrous moves—I've actually thinned out quite a lot. How much music does one actually need? I measure records in meters. A meter of one type of music is probably enough, if every record in there could be killer.

—Matt Black (Coldcut)

My record collection isn't as big as other DJs'. At one point, I wasn't DJing very much, and I sold or gave away a lot of my records. Now I probably have nine to ten crates. And those are just important records. About forty percent [of my collection] is old hip-hop that I wanted to keep: LL Cool J, historic hits like "Peter Piper" by Run DMC, or "Children's Story" by Slick Rick. I don't really do parties, so my resource of records is small.

—Rob Swift

I purge my collection a lot. But it's difficult, because music really goes in cycles. And something that doesn't sound interesting to you now might sound interesting five or ten years later. Still, there are some records that I could just do without forever.

—Peanut Butter Wolf

I go through my record collection every three to six months and pull out seventy-five percent of what I've been playing and give it back to my shop. I just moved, so I sold about two thousand of my five thousand records. Most of it was filler, the records that sound like other records. I've stripped my collection down till every record means something to me, whether it's something I loved or a classic or a great piece.

—DJ DB

I must have sold three or four thousand records in the last year. I'm getting more and more brutal as I get older. But typically, as soon as I get rid of stuff I'm back in the shop getting more. There's nothing I like better than taking a pile of old trash that I've been sent to a [shop] and exchanging four hundred dodgy promos for three or four lovely rare records.

—Jonathan More (Coldcut)

Once you've bought them, most records are worth very little, apart from to you. Out of a few thousand total, I've got about three hundred actually out in my house, and I could thin it down to about one hundred fifty I would actually bother listening to.

It's more hassle for me to sell them than just keep them. I hardly ever buy records now.

—Ben Dubuisson (Purple Penguin)

I don't know how people can get rid of them. Each track is a memory, so you don't want to lose it. You just want to lock it away somewhere.

—Kemistry (Kemistry & Storm)

I think we'd cry if we got rid of any of our records.

—Storm (Kemistry & Storm)

Have you ever been at a club and heard an incredible new song— or a version you don't recognize—yet been unable to unearth it at a record store no matter how hard you tried? (And didn't that poor clerk get exasperated over your saying, "You know, the one that goes..." before you sang four indeterminate notes?) Chances are, the tune that rocked your world was a promotional (promo) or white-label record.

To generate excitement about their releases, record labels routinely service radio stations, writers, and retailers with gratis promotional products. Since the early days of disco, club DJs have been no exception, opening their mail to find brand-new twelve-inch singles every week. This is why major label releases often clog the charts— they can afford to send out more freebies. Typically, there are several versions of a tune on a record, so if a DJ doesn't like one interpretation, there's still a likelihood he'll find another he does—as long as the damn song gets played where consumers can hear it. (There are also subscription-only services that remix tracks exclusively for release to clubs and DJs that are paying members.)

Sometimes, to build excitement among DJs and keep a record in circulation longer, mixes intended only for industry insiders—that will never be available commercially—are pressed up and sent out, too. And woe to the average Joe or Jane who falls in love with that version, although if it generates a lot of attention, it may eventually see the light of day.

> The last few years I have been deluged with around fifteen hundred promos per year. It's too many to do them all justice, and of course I can't review more than a few. It's easy to stop buying records then, but that means you end up playing the same shit as everyone else. At the moment, I buy more old music than new, which must say something.
>
> —Mixmaster Morris

Frequently, before even regular promo copies become available, what's called a white label will begin circulating. White labels are test pressings (sans printed label information, hence the term) sent out extra early to a very limited number of DJs considered arbiters of what's hot. And because they have access to these tracks, these precious few can maintain a firm grasp on their privileged status and a tune will be heard by only the patrons of select clubs for upward of months prior to a commercial release. Now and then, owing to copyright concerns like unlicensed samples, the white label is never going to be available to the public. Thus, the pursuit of these secret weapons can become a point of contention among established jocks and a source of frustration to new ones.

Even more rare are the extremely limited editions known as acetates or dubplates (although the latter term has become increasingly synonymous with white labels), a phenomenon that stretches back to the roots of DJ culture in Jamaican sound systems, when crews created acetates to outshine competitors. In the UK drum and bass scene, it's common practice for DJs to take tracks available only on DAT and press up metal acetate version, which not only costs around $50 a pop but also will last for only twenty-five to forty spins on average. (With the rise of recordable CD technology and wider availability of DAT players in clubs, some DJs predict the days of this practice are numbered.)

Ultimately, the same fundamental rules apply to promos, white labels, acetates, and so forth as any other potential material in a set. The successful integration of a track depends on the quality of the music and how the DJ programs it. But try telling that to hard-core fans of the music who always want to be one step ahead of the mainstream.

[DJs] should be judged on their merits, what they do with those tracks, rather than what [promos] they could get. But it seems to be in this country that you have to have a certain amount of new tracks in your set. If you haven't got certain tunes, you're not going to be looked at [fairly], which I think is wrong to a certain extent.

—Storm (Kemistry & Storm)

I've heard a lot of people play white label, dubplate sets that have been absolutely pointless. We've got a guy we bring over from Brazil, DJ Marky. He's hardly got any dubplates, but he scratches and he cuts up. He plays records that most people know, but he tears the house down every time.

—Jumping Jack Frost

Obviously we've got people who will give us stuff very early, but we're using dubplates as a promotional tool. The tracks that we do play, that we want to promote, are ones we really love and play very hard. We don't cut everything. And we're not hiding anything. We'll have the artist written on [the label], when it's going to come out, the label, all the information.

—Storm (Kemistry & Storm)

The whole point of a dubplate is promoting and testing the record. There are some tunes people offer me on DAT and I go, "This is absolutely terrible." But there are others that I've had on

MEET THE DJ

Jared Buckhiester

DJ DB

Since the late '80s, New York's DJ DB has been making significant contributions to the U.S. dance scene. His club NASA was one of the earliest strongholds of rave culture stateside. As A&R director for Profile's Sm:)e imprint, he introduced artists like Air Liquide, Omni Trio, and Mighty Dub Katz (alias Fatboy Slim's Norman Cook) to America's ears. And in 1996, he helped launch Breakbeat Science, the nation's first all-jungle retail vendor.

So what possible connection could such a bastion of the underground share with '80s pop acts Shannon, Eurythmics, Art of Noise, and Soul Sonic Force? The answer is Colin Faver. The weekend resident at London's Camden Palace, Faver spun them all in his sets, leaving an indelible mark on DB's twenty-year-old psyche. "It was just amazing technical mixing of all these genres," he recounts. "I used to go and stand off to the side and just watch him—wouldn't even go near the dance floor. He's the reason I DJ." Undoubtedly, there are American youngsters who voice similar sentiments today about DB.

Moving to New York in 1989, the London native ran fledgling events fueled by a mixed soundtrack reminiscent of the flourishing UK vibe. But he made his big splash in 1992, when he and his cohort Scotto launched NASA (Nocturnal Audio and Sensory Awakening). Soon exuberant young clubbers were queuing up around the block to hear the latest in uplifting breakbeat hardcore anthems.

Even after that club's conclusion, DB continued to champion America's nascent jungle scene via his Sm:)e post, spotlighting seminal cuts by 4 Hero, Aphrodite, LTJ Bukem, DJ Rap, and Photek on his *History of Our World* compilations.

These days, DB can be found by day running a new label F-111 under the auspices of Warner Bros. His latest mix CD, *Shades of Technology*, appeared on their sublabel Higher Education. Meanwhile, New Yorkers can hear him regularly at his most recent home, the weekly party PHISICS.

dubplate, and then they come out in the record shops, and six months later I'm still playing them!

—Jumping Jack Frost

Back in the '70s and '80s, having unreleased tracks was still a source of status. Because of where I was playing and my audience, I was lucky enough to have a lot of them. But I think the whole dance experience suffers because of that [phenomenon]. Introducing new music can be the best part of the night. But if something is played just because it's new and unheard, the program becomes two-dimensional.

—Robbie Leslie

If I play a record, it's got to be good. If I've got it on acetate and I don't like it, I'll say to the record company, "It's not for me. If you want the slate back, take it back." That doesn't mean I'm not into the artist or I might not play his follow-up, but I'd rather be honest. And I've got that reputation now.

—Paul Oakenfold

When a big DJ is going to another country, the people want to hear the next phase of what's going on in England. When we were in America, we found that the crowds were very happy that we played a forward-thinking set. They didn't want to hear tracks that they'd already got. They were asking for dubplates we haven't even got yet!

—Storm (Kemistry & Storm)

One way that some DJs ensure a flow of new and promo-only releases is by joining a record pool. The way it works is that certain record companies elect to provide the pool, an organization run by a pool director, with a quantity of records they want in circulation. DJs pay the pool regular dues, in exchange for which they get a box of these new tunes—which technically are free, since they're promo only—at regular intervals. The DJs have to report back to the pool director with the response of their patrons as well as their own opinions. Then the pool director compiles that information and feeds it back to the record labels, who can take the information into account when going about their nefarious marketing, promotion, and publicity campaigns.

Considering how beneficial record pools are for the labels producing the music, it's rather remarkable the practice was actually started by DJs. In 1975, Steve D'Acquisto and David Mancuso, with help from some of their colleagues (and press support from Vince Aletti at *Record World* magazine, *Billboard*'s biggest competitor at the time), launched the New York Record Pool (NYRP).

As clubs and DJs had gained popularity in the early days of disco, both record labels and DJs had noted the ability of the latter to influence a record's sales. Soon the companies releasing music began trying to influence which new songs were getting played...and by whom.

> There were a lot of clubs in those days. Let's say there was a song that everybody loved. That record was played on any given night, especially on the weekend. We were reaching a lot of people. And then they would go out and buy the records. We were doing marketing research for the record company, providing feedback and acting as a promotional thing, so they knew what horse was coming in. But we just wanted to have the records, because that's what gave us our jobs.
>
> —David Mancuso

> The reason the New York Record Pool came to be is Tony Sarafino at CTI Records wouldn't give me a copy of "What a Difference a Day Makes" by Esther Phillips. He said I wasn't big enough at the time to get a promotional twelve-inch.
>
> —Steve D'Acquisto

Although the New York DJ community in the mid-'70s was still close-knit and small—only twenty-five or so participants—favoritism threatened to create rifts between jocks who didn't need to compete for jobs. On top of all this, labels began insisting that DJs lucky enough to receive promos could pick them up only at specified times, which didn't necessarily jive with the twilight world of the clubs. After a summit between the two camps at the disco Hollywood ended in confused mayhem, D'Acquisto and Mancuso had a brainstorm, one that illustrates the unity that characterized their burgeoning scene.

All the key DJs in the city took part in the NYRP and paid only minimal dues to belong. If a label wanted a record in circulation, it had to send just enough promo copies for all the members to be serviced to Mancuso's new Prince Street Loft space. All the contributions were then distributed so everybody got the same new items simultaneously. (Originally, D'Acquisto wanted to actually charge labels a fee for the privilege of submitting music, but that notion never took hold.) In exchange for a small loss of influence over the scene, the record companies got back comments from the DJs about how the record was received.

Since the birth of the NYRP in the '70s, much has changed in the practice. Dues are more exorbitant and standards for admission in effect keep out many newcomers; on the positive side, there are now specific pools catering to DJs with specialized interests. Labels have been known to ship pools an unnecessary surplus of copies, which allows pool directors to garnish their income by selling extras to retailers, who can then mark these rarities up for resale to ordinary consumers. Or they may elect to send only a tiny few, to be doled out as treats for pool favorites.

More importantly, there are two-sided aesthetic concerns (as Mixmaster Morris hinted earlier). Belonging to a pool can mean spending less time record shopping and getting a head start on upcoming hits, but if all of a DJ's peers get the same titles at the same time, how distinctive can he or she reasonably expect to be?

Record pools started around the time...when I was at Mudd Club. The one for the white people playing new wave was Rockpool. David Azarc was the main DJ at Mudd at that time, and I was the alternate. Rockpool gave David free membership, but they wanted to charge me. I thought, *Why do I have to come to you to get the music that I've been breaking?* As soon as other DJs started playing the music I was, I'd stop playing it and would move on to something else. So I didn't join.

—Anita Sarko

Before we started getting promotional product in the early '70s, we were buying our own records. That was the best time because we actually chose the things [we played]; they weren't handed to us. You'd spend a lot more time living in record shops. We didn't have to pull a diamond out of the batch of shit they were giving us.

—Steve D'Acquisto

It should be noted that record pools are a uniquely American phenomenon. In England, if you're not serviced directly by the record label with an advance or promotional copy, your only alternative is to buy one in the shops like everyone else. But at least then you know what you're getting....

[The record pool] is a concept that people don't know in England.
—Storm (Kemistry & Storm)

That's a bit too diplomatic for some DJs to be able to handle.
—Kemistry (Kemistry & Storm)

When we used to run the Metalheadz mailing list, people had to work very hard to get on. If somebody was very big or they felt they should be on that mailing list, they couldn't just automatically have

MEET THE DJ

Kate Auleta

Jumping Jack Frost

Any drum and bass disciple with sufficient discipline to stop dancing during a Jumping Jack Frost set—no easy feat, mind you—and listen critically to his programming wouldn't be astonished to learn that Frost's roots lie in funk, soul, and disco. After inheriting a relative's record collection, he began spinning in his teens and was already emerging as a pirate radio DJ when he discovered house music in the late '80s.

Over the course of his career, Frost has embraced a variety of sounds, connecting the dots between acid house, hardcore, and drum and bass. "Most of the records that I play are made by people with the same kind of background as me," explains the London native. "The music I play now goes right back to where I started from, but it's more modern: we've got the breaks, the computerized sounds. My sets have come full circle, but [are] enhanced for the computer age."

The same expansive aesthetic informs his own productions (including "The Burial" by Leviticus), and his A&R decisions for V Recordings, the label he founded in 1993 with cohort Bryan Gee. Having launched with releases by Bristol kingpins Roni Size and Krust, their outstanding track record is captured on the *V Classic Volumes 1 & 2* compilations. The recent *Planet V* collection (which takes its title from the successful V Recordings New York City club night) featured exclusive contributions from a who's who of top-notch artists, including Ed Rush & Optical, Dillinjah, Adam F, and Lemon D.

"We enjoy what we do and seeing people happy," says Frost of the V posse's trans-Atlantic success. "I love being in [New York's] Twilo, or Brazil, or in L.A. on my first trip to America, and seeing someone with a V tattoo. Those are the things that drive us. We have photographs of all those people in our office!"

[the records]. There were people who didn't get on the Metalheadz mailing list for a good two or three years, and when they did, we knew they were going to play everything, because they'd phone every week.

—Storm (Kemistry & Storm)

I've never really understood record pools. When I first moved to the United States, a couple of people suggested that I join [one]. You had to do a little interview, be DJing a certain amount of nights per week...and pay the pool quite a considerable amount of money as well. So I joined. And was horrified to find I was getting piles of unlistenable promo rubbish!

—DJ DB

MEET THE DJ

Mixmaster Morris

"There's so much fascinating modern music out there, I don't know how DJs manage to play such boring shit," lamented England's Mixmaster Morris back in 1995. This self-appointed "international cheerleader" of ambient music may draw catcalls for his outspoken opinions and fashion-forward sensibility (it takes a special breed to sport a holographic suit...especially in a hot, sweaty club), his impeccable musical taste defies detractors.

Although he first manned the decks back in 1980, Morris didn't truly begin his rise to prominence until five years later, when he took to the airwaves with *The Mongolian Hip Hop Show*. His visions for acid house performances crystalized with the Madhouse, widely regarded as London's first live techno shindig, in 1988, and soon led to the celebrated Synergy parties alongside the Shamen.

Disillusioned with the rave scene, in the early '90s Morris began trafficking in chill-out music via unconventional events like Telepathic Fish (an "ambient tea party") and Spacetime. His motivation, then as now, was purely aesthetic. "When I started doing ambient music, the idea that you could be paid for it was hysterical."

A recording artist, too, Morris has made three groundbreaking albums as the Irresistible Force: *Flying High, Global Chillage,* and most recently, *It's Tomorrow Already*. He's also collaborated with fellow pioneers Pete Namlook and Jonah Sharp. Of his two mix CDs, 1996's *The Morning After* brews an interesting blend of laid-back jungle and woozy hip-hop beats, and his split *Mixmag* disc with the Orb's Alex Patterson is considered an ambient masterpiece.

Mixmaster Morris also writes regularly in the music press, publicizing groundbreaking artists, including Aphex Twin, Black Dog, and Squarepusher early in their careers. But his thought-provoking DJ sets remain his greatest outlet for promoting new sounds. "I always believed music was for sharing with people," he says today. "We hear so much shit commercial music that we must do all we can to redress the balance."

6 It Takes Two

There are certain laws and physics to the art of DJing that we all respect and live by. You've got to know how to match two records, how to blend. And that will give you a sense of tempo, of speed. You've got to know the basics. You keep those laws for reference, and then you build on that.

—Rob Swift

Rule number one: Never let the music stop.

—David Mancuso

Separating the intertwined disciplines of mixing and programming into distinct entities is as delicate (and controversial) a procedure as dividing conjoined twins. Where the lines are drawn differs from DJ to DJ; some don't delineate between the two at all. Rather than get bogged down in semantics, let's say—just for now—that mixing is primarily concerned with *how* you play one record after another, whereas programming (addressed in the next two chapters) is *why* you play the music you do, when you do.

As DJ culture has proliferated internationally, an increasing amount of attention surrounding the craft has focused on the mixing finesse of whoever's manning the wheels of steel, particularly in the good old US of A.

We've always been conscious of the standard of DJing in America. We've played with loads of local [U.S.] DJs who aren't big names but are technically a lot better than big name DJs in England.
—Ed Simons (The Chemical Brothers)

I got fed up and walked away from the whole game in the mid-'80s. People were putting all the emphasis on the mix, and not the six minutes of music that were gonna come after it.
—Steve D'Acquisto

In this environment, it's not shocking that a lot of aspiring DJs place great emphasis on mixing from one track to the next seamlessly. If you want to keep the music playing continuously in an exciting fashion, ultimately you're going to have to move through a variegated program. That entails creating segues via alternate means besides synching up beats.

Be aware that different musical camps favor distinct approaches to mixing. In drum and bass or hip-hop the transitions are much quicker, whereas in trance or house sets the DJ often extends the layered intersection between cuts into an expressive moment of its own.

There are different mixing techniques in hip-hop and house, obviously. Hip-hop is more abrupt, with the scratching. It's more about showmanship and less about blending. With house, you're taking them on a musical ride. You can go hard with some tribal, and then get soft and happy with vocals. You can lift them up so high, then back down, then right back up. It's like a big roller coaster.
—DJ Skribble

Regardless of your musical program, dexterity, concentration and physical precision are all essential for polished mixing. But unless there's a musical aesthetic underpinning your transitions, they'll lack that little something extra that elevates a set above the ordinary.

The master key to effectively mixing any music is to know the records you're playing inside and out. That shouldn't be a chore, right? After all, a desire to share the music they love with others is the main reason most folks start DJing. If you really care passionately about the tunes you're playing, mixing should almost be a secondary concern.

> It's all about going out and buying the records and being into them myself. There are plenty of DJs who don't do any mixing but can move a crowd.
>
> —Ben Dubuisson (Purple Penguin)

> Back in '91, we were just doing our own parties. There really was no scene. It wasn't like I said, "I want to be a DJ" and was struggling to beat mix. I had a musical background, so timing came naturally to me, but [being a DJ] wasn't about technical skill at that point. It was more like, "Hey, let's have a party, and we'll go to this person's house and set up turntables. . . ." There was never pressure or competition. We just wanted to play good music for each other.
>
> —Heather Heart

> When I'm going from the tail end of one record to the beginning of another, I just do it in the air. I can hear it. I do it in a way that is more sonic, like a little blend, nothing to do with beats or anything. I'm not into that.
>
> —David Mancuso

Get accustomed to listening to records as a unified piece of music as well as interlocking components. Back in the dawn of beat matching, the knowledge DJs required of every record in their crate was even more intimate than it is today. They had to be aware of the instrumentation within a track, the fidelity and dynamics of the record, and the harmonic structure of the song. They also had to stay on top of tempos that weren't fixed. Before new wave, house, and techno made electronic drums commonplace, DJs had to accommodate the whims of human drummers (and people who hit things for a living aren't notoriously reliable—ask Keith Moon).

> When I started listening to music, records were musical instruments. It was about listening to the whole orchestra of sound and respecting everything from the strings to the horns to the keyboards to the drums and cymbals. It was as though somebody ran over a band and flattened them, and you had to reconstitute them. You knew every element in that band and how to deal with them all.
>
> —Peter Calandra

> From the time I was five or six years old, my mother had me taking every kind of music lesson they had. When I started DJing, I knew all about structure and keys and arrangement. So it was a lot easier to put together records that should be together musically, that aren't dissonant, and transition smoothly, like a regular key change in a normal record.
>
> —Jesse Saunders

> There's no computerized drumbeat [on old records] to help you out. You have to be really familiar with each tempo and understand the nuances in each rhythm to be really effective.
>
> —Peter Calandra

> You'll be playing a record where the drummer tries, but he still can't keep the tempo exact for a whole record, and he drifts. That's a nightmare to mix. If you could mix those records, you can mix anything together.
>
> —Jesse Saunders

MEET THE DJ

Jesse Saunders

Sometimes being an innovator doesn't pay. An invention can revolutionize the world even while the ersatz Einstein behind it goes unrecognized. Since the mid-'80s, house music has exerted an expanding sphere of influence internationally. But do you know who released the first house record?

Jesse Saunders was born on the south side of Chicago in March 1962. By the tender age of seven, Jesse had begun buying singles. Later he began making mix tapes and primitive edits of his favorite tunes. In high school, he and his stepbrother Wayne Williams convinced their cousin, a successful DJ, to let them play at local dances, where Jesse's homemade extended versions proved a surprise hit.

Spinning a mix that reached beyond the funk and disco favorites, Saunders rose slowly through the Chicago club scene of the late '70s and early '80s. As resident DJ at the Playground, he often worked upward of ten hours a night. His signature track was a bootleg featuring snippets of Donna Summer's "Bad Girls," Lipps Inc's "Funkytown," and the bass line from "Space Invaders," which Jesse would augment with a drum machine. When his secret weapon was stolen during a break-in, Jesse decided to create his own studio version. The new "On and On"—the very first house record—was released via his Jes Say Records in January 1984.

A slew of similar releases from other Chicago DJ-producers followed. Jesse had a hand in several, most notably Farley "Jackmaster" Funk's "Love Can't Turn Around" (which he wrote and produced). But he slowed down his DJ career to concentrate on writing and producing. Later he relocated to Southern California, focusing on other aspects of the music business...even as house exploded in England.

In 1994, after a ten-year hiatus, Jesse resumed DJing regularly. He was surprised by some of the changes. "Back in the '80s, if I got two hundred dollars in a night to DJ, that was a big night!" Among his many enterprises, Saunders is the author of *House Music...The Real Story*, his account of the genre's ascent from the Chicago underground to international acclaim.

Beat matching, one of the most popular methods of mixing, involves segueing two records of relatively similar tempos together, making adjustments in speed up or down (using the deck's pitch control or your finger), keeping them synchronized as you use the fader to blend them. The quaint term for when you attempt to do this and fail is *train wreck*. The first time you hear this happen, you'll understand.

The tempo of records is measured in beats per minute, or bpm. Many jocks use a digital metronome or similar device to clock the bpm of each of their records, then note the tempo on the record or sleeve itself for easy reference.

> When I first met the Coldcut boys in '85, I was amazed that they could tell the bpm of a track instantly. I started annotating all my records with bpm, something I still do today.
>
> —Mixmaster Morris

> Back [in the mid-'80s], you couldn't have a box of house records that all mixed together smoothly, because they're within two or three bpm of each other. Everyone was playing many different genres. You had stuff that was one hundred bpm and stuff that went up to one hundred forty, from really slow British electro to crazy-fast Sisters of Mercy and Sigue Sigue Sputnik records. The resident Camden Palace DJ had this incredible system. Within five bpm, like one hundred to one hundred five, he would call that "A." And one hundred five to one hundred ten, he'd call "B." He had everything up to J. I thought this was genius. You could just pull the letters out.
>
> —DJ DB

> I remember one time at the record pool, this guy walked in and was talking about a beat book [an index of songs organized by bpm]. This was when the whole beats-per-minute idea came in.

And we laughed at him. "What are you talking about? This is totally unnecessary!" But it became very popular.

—David Mancuso

It's become more common to just align rhythm tracks from one record to the next and not concentrate on content or direction or drama. That's the evolution of the art form.

—Robbie Leslie

Naturally, the faster the records are spinning, the sooner they'll go their separate ways if the DJ doesn't pay attention.

The bpm factor is a big consideration when you're mixing hard-core, especially up around two hundred fifty or two hundred sixty bpm. The bass lines are going so quick, they start to rub up together, and the beat becomes muddy. That's where knowing the record well has a lot to do with solid mixing.

—DJ Tron

Mixing doesn't begin and end with bpm. You don't need a master's degree in orchestral conducting to recognize when songs don't sound right together, even at the exact same speed. Perhaps they're in keys that don't harmonically mesh pleasantly, or one record is pressed better, so the sound is more crisp and vibrant. Sometimes you can use a mixer to adjust EQ levels and smooth out these differences; sometimes you can't. Think of it this way—you can dress a drag queen up in a sensible Ann Taylor ensemble, but if she's six feet four inches tall and broad shouldered, she'll attract attention regardless.

You have to consider how the record was mastered, how loud the pressing is, and the fidelity. That's something you just acquire knowledge of. For example, take "Come On, Dance, Dance" by the Saturday Night Band, released on Prelude in the

MEET THE DJ

Liam Howlett of the Prodigy

Could you pick Liam Howlett out of a police lineup?

His band, the Prodigy, was responsible for the MTV smash "Firestarter" and a number one album, 1997's *Fat of the Land*. If any single group merits applause for dispelling the American myth that all dance acts are faceless, those hand-claps belong to this UK quartet who've been pop mainstays at home since their 1981 rave anthem "Charly."

"That's him, officer!" you shout triumphantly. "The one with the pointy Day-Glo hair and face piercings!" Wrong. You've mistakenly fingered acrobatic madman Keith Flint. Howlett, the musical genius behind the act, usually hangs at the back of the action, hiding his foxy features behind a battery of keyboards and computers while his three cohorts aerobicize downstage.

But long before anyone anywhere recognized the Prodigy, Liam Howlett was a hip-hop DJ. "In 1986, at fifteen years old, I worked all through my summer holidays to save up for two turntables." The same year, he entered Capital Radio's Mixmaster of the Year. But after submitting his three-minute entry cassette, he decided it wasn't good enough. So he tried again, using a pseudonym. "And I won first and third place! I took that as a sign."

Recently, Howlett returned to his roots with *Prodigy Presents... The Dirtchamber Sessions, Volume One*, a staggering old-school mishmash where Howlett forges everything from Jane's Addiction to LL Cool J into a galvanized party monster of a CD. Prodigy fans might be taken aback by the program, but they shouldn't be. "All I was trying to do was have an album that incorporates records that were important to me at different stages in my life," says Howlett with a grin. And in doing so, he's created yet another Prodigy title that promises to serve a similar function for millions of new listeners.

mid-'70s. That record's got a very weak drum, it's compressed and tinny, and it doesn't have a lot of dynamics. Contrast that with "Knock On Wood" by Amii Stewart, which is like a diesel locomotive coming through the club. But that's a burlesque example—those two records don't go together.

—Robbie Leslie

Obviously, you've got to watch the old bass drum [levels] or they'll cancel each other out when they come in time.

—Liam Howlett

When I mix, it's very pleasant to listen to. . . . I like to be able to pick each sound out. There's nothing I hate more than people who just carelessly mix two records together with no thought to what's going on.

—DJ Rap

If the DJs aren't attentive and careful, they run the risk of compromising the music in pursuit of the "perfect" mix. (Some might argue that this isn't as great a concern with records made by DJ-producer types, who come from a background that takes into consideration such practices as pitching records up or down to match beats when recording.) Superlative club and party jocks traditionally aim to incorporate the aesthetics of the original recording artists into their own overall agenda.

Let the tunes play. Someone's taken the time to make the record—at least let a bit of it play. The best DJs are like that; they do a bit of cutting and then they play some tunes.

—Ben Dubuisson (Purple Penguin)

Try to have a situation where whatever the artist intended sonically gets through when you play records. If you do anything that interferes with that, then it's not about the music, it's

MEET THE DJ

DJ Rap

Some hopefuls become DJs to rack up frequent-flyer miles and see the world, but not London's DJ Rap. Charissa Saverio grew up in luxury hotels in Africa and Asia before her folks decided to ship her off to assorted boarding schools and convents. She spent much of her teens backpacking around Europe.

So when acid house exploded in England, Charissa was working at a law firm and dating an ordinary guy, assembling something resembling a normal life. "But I had these two friends—wacked out on acid." This dynamic duo insisted the scene was calling Charissa's name, and one night, after a particularly big blowout with the boyfriend, she took the bait. "So I went to this rave, took my first pill..." Within a matter of days, Saverio was single, unemployed, a squatter, and raving nonstop.

Collecting records and learning the skills soon followed, once she'd gotten her first taste of hardcore. Concurrently, she began making her own tracks. After cutting the classic "Ambience—the Adored" with a neophyte producer in 1990, she found herself promoting the tune on pirate radio, where she picked up a few more mixing tricks and DJ Rap was born. After a handful of small gigs, she landed her first real shot one night when Fabio missed a slot and a promoter she'd been pestering relented.

Through the '90s DJ Rap has risen through the ranks to become one of the UK drum and bass scene's mainstays. Her productions—1993's "Spiritual Aura," 1995's "Roughest Gunark"—consistently deliver the goods, while her pumping sets anchor liquid melodies with blistering breakbeats. She also runs the labels Proper Talent and Low Key, releasing her debut LP Intelligence in 1993 via the latter. Most recently, she launched a full-scale assault on U.S. shores with her second album, *Learning Curve*. And the passport stamps keep piling up....

about your ego. The sensationalism and the excitement of the record should be left up to the artist.

—David Mancuso

You want to be exciting and do something different to the tracks that makes people want to come hear you. But by the same token, you should have enough respect for artists to not mess their record up totally. Especially tracks with vocals. There's only so far you can pitch up a vocal before it starts sounding like Alvin and the Chipmunks.

—Juan Atkins

I've learned to just let the songs speak for themselves. My style is mainly to get people dancing, to have a good time. A big part of that is just exposing them to the music and trying to get the mixes nice and smooth.

—Peanut Butter Wolf

Please take your time and let me appreciate the record. If somebody brings in a record too soon, I'm like, "Oh my God, I bet he comes quickly in bed." You just know that person can't fuck.

—DJ Rap

Ideally, a DJ's mixing skills ultimately become more of an aesthetic consideration than a matter of technical nuts and bolts, adding to but not overshadowing the music.

For us, it's all about being tight in the mix and making everything work musically. We don't do any tricks—we don't scratch, we don't cut, we just do basic mixing. More than any other kind of music, drum and bass is about a plain mixing kind of style. It's what you're doing in that mix that makes you dramatic.

—Storm (Kemistry & Storm)

You're mixing two tracks, and making a new one in the middle.
—Kemistry (Kemistry & Storm)

I met a Jamaican DJ once called Marvelous Marvin. He played in England once and changed my life. Do you remember that [George Kranz] track, "Din Da Da"? And then the old funky drum and bass track "Let the Drummer Get Wicked"? This guy did a mix of those two that made me rush like I had never rushed. After that mix he went on to drop an a cappella of Soul II Soul's "It's So Tough" on top of "Pacific" by 808 State. I learned then about records being in tune with each other. He taught me how to create a remix. Anyone can mix, but how about creating something really beautiful with two records together?
—DJ Rap

The easiest thing is to just play back the data. The harder thing is to modify that data and make it work with other things. By using EQ or effects, you can decide which data to cross over between the two sources. That's where it becomes a musical art form.
—Richie Hawtin (Plastikman)

But how does one learn to do all this? Sadly, through such old-fashioned means as observation, application, and practice. Or brokering a trade with Satan. The process of learning to make your records and your hands generate the sounds you can hear in your brain over the speakers can be maddening. But here are a few helpful pointers from the experts, along with pitfalls to be aware of.

Don't give up! You're not going to mix right away. Don't throw your turntables out the window, don't sell them, and don't smash your records. It's going to happen; you've just got to give it time.
—DJ Tron

Was I patient? Oh no! Records were flying everywhere. I've never actually broken a record, but I will throw them. It was an incredibly frustrating time. I would always mix with two of my favorite tunes so I would remain happy. It would take me the whole record to get to the end, and then you'll be "in" for a minute. But once you get it, you get it, and that's it.

—DJ Rap

The tracks were everything. If I listened to a track and was moved by it, I didn't see why other people shouldn't be.

—Ben Dubuisson (Purple Penguin)

I learned fairly quickly how to beat match. But it took a good three or four years before I realized that beat matching wasn't the really important part; it was the structure of the track, the eight beats to the bar business. That took me a long time to figure out. And it took a lot longer to develop that internal clock that's always counting the [bars of] eight [beats], where you don't even think about that anymore.

—DJ DB

Early on, I learned that there was a whole science of eight-on-eight that needs to be employed. You're spelling something out, making a sentence out of two records, and that doesn't happen by chance. [It's] engineered. Say the song you're playing is going to end with a triple chorus that's thirty-two—thirty-two—thirty-two—[beats per chorus]. And your next one starts with eight—sixteen, and then you have a vocal. If you want to play out all of those three choruses, when you're into the third one and the first eight beats expire, you get that next puppy launched.

—Peter Calandra

Get access to decks and your own little space. And don't be afraid of touching your records. We didn't touch our records for ages.

—Storm (Kemistry & Storm)

It's really important to make tapes and listen to yourself playing. You'll listen back to a tape and go, "Ooh, that's terrible," but you realize what you're doing. Mixing is a natural thing, and it comes, and you get your own style and develop it.

—DJ Rap

Everything sounds great in the bedroom. Then you go out and it's a whole new world. Everything's that much [farther] away, and that much louder . . . and there's that much more adrenaline running through your body!

—Barry Ashworth

If you're still practicing in a year's time and you really believe in it, then you might not be the best DJ, but you're one step in the right direction.

—Richie Hawtin (Plastikman)

Regardless of the type of music you love or the mixing style you employ, one of the easiest ways to develop your chops is by working with two copies of the same record. It makes breaking down the components and then learning how to reassemble them much less intimidating. (And having an instrumental version of a particularly tricky vocal track can help build a bridge to your next selection.)

I always used to buy two copies of records that had a cappella tracks or instrumentals or just beats, so I could make DJ–b-boy tapes for me and my friends to listen to. One of my favorite things I used to do was cutting up this Hijack track called "Doomsday of

Rap." It had an instrumental b side and an a cappella as well. You could cut in the a cappella and learn scratching techniques.

—Liam Howlett

Records designed for dance floor play have the needs and practices of DJs in mind. But they're still unique creations first, and the most exciting ones usually don't follow all—or any—of "the rules." DJs who rely exclusively on records that follow cut-and-dried formulas often spin sets that resemble playing with Legos more than using prerecorded music creatively. The DJ who knows every element of a record in his or her crate and how DJ-friendly each one is is better prepared to navigate tricky mixes.

The structure of the mix is very important. A lot of times it's unfriendly to bring [a song] in at the beginning, if you want to keep something going in a smooth way. On older records, instrumental passages and breakdowns are sometimes located in the middle. So if you want to be discreet, you have to start there and then hook up choruses or vamps [with a second copy] and take it up to the top that way.

—Robbie Leslie

I create records, and everything you need is all in the mix. You can make a record with a nice intro, but do a mix that starts out with the kick [drum] or some [hand] claps, something that's going to keep the DJs on the one. Because believe me, there [are] a lot of DJs out there [who] don't know where the one is on a record!

—Juan Atkins

If a record doesn't start with "boom-boom-boom," DJs can't mix it in. That's why there's no fancy mixing anymore. That's one thing I learned from doing remixes. You've got to give them a million bars of "boom-boom-boom."

—Kurtis Mantronik

MEET THE DJ

Barry Ashworth of Dub Pistols

Barry Ashworth is not a timid soul. If one look at his rugged yet lovable mug isn't evidence enough, lend an ear to his robust sets or *Point Blank,* the premiere platter from his group, Dub Pistols. Or take a gander at his résumé.

Our story begins in 1987, with a broken leg—Barry's a bit accident prone—a bar brawl in Majorca, and an escape to Ibiza. Ashworth's island getaway opened the door to new avenues of wonderful trouble, and when he returned to London he began promoting parties.

Back then Ashworth kept the jam pumping from everywhere but behind the turntables. He let his younger brother assume that mantle, so long as Barry could practice on the family Technics. As a promoter, he was responsible for two of London's most deliciously denominated clubs, Eat the Worms and Naked Lunch. Meanwhile, his old band Déjà Vu aimed to be London's answer to Happy Mondays or Stone Roses.

When the DJ bug finally bit, Barry manned the decks in his own backrooms. "I just played whatever I wanted, without being too serious. But I'd be so fucking nervous, I used to get on, put a couple records on, pass out on to the decks, and get carried off after about two tracks...literally." Eventually he learned to keep it together for a whole set, and bookings followed.

After their remix of Monkey Mafia's "Blow the Whole Joint Up" caught the attention of UK record execs, Ashworth's new outfit, the Dub Pistols, was signed to DeConstruction's Concrete imprint in 1996. Although Ashworth's bombastic melange on the ones-and-twos and with his band mashes up the energy of punk with techno, soul, and dub textures, Barry bristles at being tagged big beat. "I won't buy into [genres], because as soon as you do, you've gone from being the latest thing to the worst thing, and you're back down at the bottom of the pile."

[New records] are like an instant brownie mix. You basically have everything broken down precisely. But that's not so with a lot of old records. Think of old KC and the Sunshine Band records—you're lucky if you got sixteen beats before they started in!

—Peter Calandra

Despite what a lot of mainstream club DJs would have people think, beat matching isn't the alpha and omega of mixing. There are dozens of other ways to connect records. You can just drop a track in on the beat, a la early disco DJs. Or wait till a record ends cold, then start with a new one at a different speed. Or blend ambient instrumental intros and codas together. Even house or techno DJs who exclusively beat-match in extended mixes can break up their sets by cutting back and forth between records abruptly now and then, as many drum-and-bass DJs do.

It's not always about perfect mixing. Some of the best reactions I get when I'm DJing are just "Bang! Drop in the tune!"

—Andy Smith

Initially I developed this technique I refer to as "slurping." It wasn't quite beat mixing and it wasn't quite in-tune mixing. You tried to find a combination of two records where you could slip out of one and into the other without people noticing. It was only in the later stages, when DJ technique became so all encompassing, that I started thinking that I ought to learn how to beat mix.

—Jonathan More (Coldcut)

Depending on what I'm doing, sometimes I won't even mix at the end of the set. A lot of drum and bass songs end and start the same way—you don't even have to mix them. Sometimes you can just wait till the right break comes along, when you've got some nice music, and you can drop something else in. Or you can cut off the turntable and let the record slow down by itself, nice and slow.

—Juan Atkins

You don't have to beat-match every mix, and you don't have to slam every mix, and you don't have to melt every mix. I like to do a blend of it all.

—DJ Tron

Some DJs even use unconventional sounds to bridge songs, for aesthetic and technical reasons. Larry Levan and Chicago house legend Frankie Knuckles both slipped sound effects in between songs, to modify the crowd's energy and signal a change in musical direction without making a jarring shift. Spoken word tracks or samples can be useful in this fashion, too. Want to make a trip-hop set really creepy? Screw Tricky—drop an excerpt from *Sylvia Plath Reading Her Own Poetry*. Even nonmusical recordings can add a new dimension to a narrative implied by the lyrical flow of a set.

When I first started DJing, trying to fit together the records that I liked was quite difficult sometimes. A lot of DJs at that time talked between records, but I hated that and found it particularly embarrassing. So I started looking for records that started with phrases. Then when I got stuck and couldn't mix from one to the other, because of tuning or whatever, I used to drop one of my patent records with a phrase. Then I could escape into another area.

—Jonathan More (Coldcut)

As the parameters of DJ culture continue to expand, some pioneers—like Alec Empire, Christian Marclay, and DJ Spooky—have abandoned or radically minimized traditional mixing practices in their work. By combining a wide range of unfamiliar sonic materials

MEET THE DJ

DJ Tron

Gabba, speedcore, bouncy techno, terrorcore. The genre names may change, but nobody is innocent, and there is no protection. Especially when the one in charge is Chicago's DJ Tron, one of the biggest names in hardcore.

Before discovering the Midwest rave scene in the early '90s, his musical tastes ran a bit differently. "I was into punk: Bad Religion, Pennywise, Minor Threat, the Misfits," he reveals. Later he began exploring dance clubs. "I started listening to Front 242, Nitzer Ebb, and Frontline Assembly, the whole Wax Trax! sound. From then on, I liked digital music." The two styles hardly seemed incongruous. "Whether you're at a punk rock or [an] industrial show, there's always a [mosh] pit, there's always action," Tron observes. "There's aggression to the music."

Once he'd embraced techno, his rapid descent into the depths of hardcore seemed inevitable. After a few years of private practice, Tron landed his first rave slot. Although his sets today boast considerable variety, his debut was distinguished by a merciless onslaught of the hardest sounds available. "People really responded to that, they got into it."

Although some argue that America's youth are wasting their lives with TV and video games, they've made DJ Tron the man he is today. "Watching movies all my life, especially sci-fi and horror movies, has influenced everything I've done. I like a lot of the dark soundscapes in those movies, so I try to play records that have a darker edge to them."

For further illustration, check out *Chrome Padded Cell*, his surprisingly engaging, albeit exhausting program of experimental hardcore. Like a good horror film director, Tron sets up expectations, then postpones them, delivering the brutal coup de grace only once defenses have been dropped. "I'll end a song abruptly, begin with something completely shocking, and do ridiculous things throughout that nobody would expect," he says with a laugh. "I want to be the David Lynch of techno."

in ways that eschew not only DJ convention but Western musical practice as well, they can fashion new sonic hybrids of jarring, thought-provoking impact.

> When I was first in the techno underground, I wasn't into copying American hip-hop technique. Those guys would scratch and do it really well. We were working more with fading stuff in and out instead, doing layers of beats. But when I left the techno scene, I thought, *Okay, there is something about [mixing] that could be really developed.* Keep that approach of putting two tracks on top of each other for a longer period of time—longer than hip-hop DJs do—plus add scratches in an anarchist way.
>
> —Alec Empire

> In the beginning I was into complete dissonance, rhythms clashing. Especially on my college radio show. Public Enemy samples this old James Brown track, "Blow Your Head," and I would mix the original over the Public Enemy [track], playing at the wrong speed. And then I'd have two or three CD players with discs skipping and weird loops. It sounded like total chaos going out on the air. But people who were into hip-hop thought it was hilarious, so they'd listen.
>
> —DJ Spooky

And despite David Mancuso's admonition at the beginning of this chapter, sometimes the most effective musical moment a DJ can introduce into the mix is . . . silence.

> There's a song in my heart that goes on forever. Sometimes I do have a pause, for an effect—because sometimes a record will end cold. Then there's that little air stroke. It's silence, but it's part of the picture. And then boom, you go into the next moment.
>
> —David Mancuso

MEET THE DJ

Philipp Virus

Alec Empire of Atari Teenage Riot

Despite the emotional immediacy of dance music, the medium is rarely utilized as a political platform. "A lot of DJs come from a disco background, making Hi-NRG and house music, and no one really thinks about using statements in tracks," observes Berlin's Alec Empire. If his output as a musician, producer, and DJ seems unrelentingly didactic, bear in mind he's compensating for twenty-plus years of negligence.

Empire's band Atari Teenage Riot (ATR) has served up blistering, breakneck beats and staccato slogans like "Start the Riot" and "Destroy 2000 Years of Culture" since 1992. Meanwhile, his Digital Hardcore Recordings label provides an outlet for equally committed souls like Shizuo, Nic Endo, EC8OR, and Bomb 20. Needless to say, his DJ sets don't resemble the Hot Club Play chart for anywhere in the known universe ... except perhaps hell.

Empire's initial infatuation with DJs came via one genre that did carry political content: hip-hop. Alec's epiphany occurred after hearing Grandmaster Flash & The Furious Five's "The Message" on the radio, followed by a translation of the lyric's vivid depiction of ghetto life. "Okay," he said, "this really means something."

In his teens, Alec moved rapidly through punk and then acid house; the latter made such a strong initial impression that he began recording his own tracks and DJing. His first German release, 1992's "SuEcide 1-3" EP, is considered one of the first pure breakbeat records from outside of England. As techno became increasingly compromised by concessions to the mainstream, he broke from the herd again, forming ATR as a reaction against rising racism in the reunified Germany.

Today, Empire's sets make stylistic connections between punk rock, dub, techno, and jungle with alarming, thought-provoking abrasiveness. "A DJ is defined as someone who really, seriously puts stuff together in a creative way," he insists. "But nowadays it has become like when my parents said, 'Oh, a DJ...that's someone who plays records.'" Not if Alec Empire can help it.

Rather than keep masturbating away, until you think you've reached climax, you can pull out and stop, and start again. You can pull back from that moment of truth and make it bigger and stronger.

—Jonathan More (Coldcut)

Silence is as important as sound. You bring things down and up, take things completely away from people. It's just as important as giving people things. It's about making rules and breaking rules, changing what the people are expecting from you.

—Richie Hawtin (Plastikman)

7 Let the Music Play

A great DJ is someone who has the indefinable balance of entertainer, educator ... and flirt. Somebody who's conscientious of
what's going on with the dance floor makes a great DJ.

—DJ DB

I'm not out there to give people exactly what they want, or
something that is comfortable, all the time. I'm out there to give
them what they want and what they don't want. Hopefully you
expand someone's mind and tastes and their future.

—Richie Hawtin (Plastikman)

Programming—a sinister-sounding word for the essence of the
DJ's art—selecting what music to play and when. There are as many
approaches to programming a set as there are DJs, audiences, and
styles of music. When you start to dissect all the considerations that
go into this discipline, it's a wonder more DJs don't experience spontaneous human combustion. How much musical ground—in terms of
genres, timbres, tempos—should a set cover? How do you calibrate a
balance of old and new music? What sequence should the music follow? I can feel steam coming out of my ears right now. . . .

Rule #1, as with mixing, is the DJ should always work with music
he or she is crazy about.

You've got to love the tunes you play. If you don't like it, you know people won't react. We've all played tracks we don't like at times, thinking, *This will work*, and it does...occasionally.

—Ben Dubuisson (Purple Penguin)

If you're putting on the headphones in the record shop and thinking along the lines of *That'll really work the crowd*, that's no good. You've got to think of yourself all the time. I always think of what I would dance to. I don't dance, but if I danced, what would I dance to?

—Scott Hendy (Purple Penguin)

Always reflect your personality through your set. It's all about your personality and how you play the music.

—Jumping Jack Frost

I would rather play good music for little money than the same crap music as everybody else for big bucks. This means that I'm usually skint; credibility doesn't pay the rent. *C'est la vie.*

—Mixmaster Morris

Not surprisingly, the temptation for many DJs is to concentrate on one type of music they're rabid for. When I was a teenager, the only tunes I would shake my groove thing to were '80s synth pop tracks: Human League, Depeche Mode, Orchestral Manoeuvres in the Dark. If a DJ followed Yazoo's "Situation" with a song featuring guitars or an arrangement that erred on the side of disco, I'd exit the dance floor pronto. But a set grows tedious for both the DJ and the crowd if you don't introduce variety. As Richie Hawtin inscribed on the back of the 1995 Plastikman LP *Musik*: "Just because you like chocolate cake doesn't mean that you eat it every day."

It's better when you have all the different musical avenues coming at you. It'd be boring if you had everything just one way, all the time . . . just like if they had one whole world government.

—Afrika Bambaataa

You've got to break up the monotony, especially if you've got a three-or four-hour set. Man, you don't want to be going "boom-boom-boom" for the whole four hours.

—Juan Atkins

Give people something completely different, radically unexpected, to provoke their thought processes. Sometimes in the middle of a high-energy peak, you cut the peak off and put something completely different in the mix. In the middle of this big house set, I'll drop Lauryn Hill or A Tribe Called Quest. Next time, maybe I'll drop in Doc Scott or another drum and bass track. My function is to let people share and understand with their own body and dancing. There are other ways to dance than just this metronomic, Top 10 way.

—François K.

If people get into a groove when they're DJing, it's so easy to stay there. When I DJ, I go up and down, in peaks and troughs. Usually the guy before me is playing fast, because that's what happens in [England]. So I'll play some faster hip-hop stuff and some old funk, then gradually drop it down and get in some slow hip-hop or reggae, and then start building it back up again.

Andy Smith

The nice thing about [mixing in the early days] was every record had its own beat, so you could move in different directions. It didn't all have to be the same beat, like it is now.

—Steve D'Acquisto

Striking just the right balance of musical variety, selecting songs that people will recognize and respond to promptly, as well as new or lesser-known ones that they might like, requires a unique brand of DJ moxie that is equal parts intuition, common sense, and sheer bravado. Being pointlessly eclectic is almost as limiting as playing twenty-five 120 bpm house tracks back-to-back.

> There's a very fine line between self-indulgence and recognizing that if you put yourself out into a creative milieu, you owe something to the people that have paid to come have a good time. I will drive people off a dance floor, but I can't do it all night long. And I can't just drive them off the dance floor because I want to stand there with my head up my own butt. There has to be a rationale.
>
> —Anita Sarko

> It's a combination of playing things they're going to know and stuff that they might not have heard before. And at the end of the night, they'll go, "Oh, I heard that classic track . . . . And what was that one that went like that? I'll have to try [to] get that tomorrow." If you've done that, it's been a good night.
>
> —Andy Smith

> That's the secret to being a good DJ: a balance of education with entertainment. Bringing in a new record that you know will be a hit in six months, and people will even think, *I heard that record there first.*
>
> —Paul Oakenfold

> Don't come in just banging your own personal picks or old classics that nobody knows. Give 'em what they want first, and then they'll let you take 'em wherever you want to go.
>
> —Juan Atkins

MEET THE DJ

Patrick McMullan

Anita Sarko

Anita Sarko has always had the killer instinct, but back in the '70s law school didn't agree with the Michigan native. She relocated to Atlanta, where relatives urged her to work in her real field of expertise. "I didn't realize I knew so much, because I come from Detroit," she demurs. "Everybody in Detroit knows music."

She applied for a job at a college radio station. The minute she spoke in her low, unaccented voice, personnel insisted the only opening was for a DJ. Sarko distinguished herself quickly—"because nobody had ever heard a woman before who knew music, and my tastes were very hard. I was well known for playing [the Velvet Underground's] 'Sister Ray,' and Iggy Pop and the MC5." Observing her following, commercial stations began courting her, too.

But by 1979, Sarko was fed up with reprimands for her no-bullshit attitude. A visit to New York brought her to the Mudd Club. Appalled by the DJ's choices, she decided she could do better. She made an audition tape, packed her bags, and moved to New York City . . . sans employment.

That first tape mysteriously disappeared, but eventually she convinced owner Steve Maas to test her out, and she became a permanent fixture. Instead of status quo disco, she spun everything from post-punk by Magazine to easy listening—whatever fit the club's bizarre, distaff dynamic.

Sarko cut a swath through New York club culture, working at Danceteria and Area. When Steve Rubell opened Palladium in 1985, he tapped Anita for his exclusive Michael Todd room, where she enjoyed free rein to play whatever she pleased: Latin and African music, hip-hop, gospel. Even as Palladium's star dimmed, bookings for big parties and fashion shows filled her calendar. "When *Vanity Fair* did a piece on '80s nightlife, I was the only DJ whose trajectory they followed."

Today, Sarko is retired from DJing, devoting her energies to coordinating music for Banana Republic and magazine writing, including *Paper*'s "Auntie Anita Says" column. She's begun producing and remixing other artists and was recently enlisted to put her creative stamp on the back catalog of Petula Clark.

You can be playing brand new hip-hop records all night, and the crowd might not be responding. Then all of the sudden you go back and throw on [House of Pain's] "Jump Around" and they go nuts. Then you've got them up. So stay on that vibe for a few minutes. Then when you go back to the new stuff, they'll appreciate it.

—DJ Skribble

I lost interest in the rave scene when the DJs started to play for themselves and their mates. It wasn't as much of a buzz anymore, because you weren't hearing a certain track come in that you recognized—even if it was just a small section of the track mixing in and out. A DJ should always play a few anthems in a night and drop in some obscure stuff. But I wouldn't just throw on the token track to try [to] be cool.

—Liam Howlett

I use what I call the throw-'em-a-bone method. I'm playing to a whole new generation and the majority of them don't know [classic disco]. So I play new, popular stuff that I enjoy and know will get people onto the dance floor. Once I've got them in a groove, I'll find something that complements [the contemporary song] from a generation that I knew. All of the sudden they're in it, and they're liking it. Then I'll give them another one of their records . . . and then two of mine . . . and I'll gradually decrease the ratio.

—Peter Calandra

I like to go through my whole collection every month or so and find [older] things. You don't want to play something that was really big six months ago, because everybody's tired of it. But if it's from four or five years ago, they'll go, "Oh yeah—I forgot this song!"

—Peanut Butter Wolf

MEET THE DJ

DJ Skribble

Growing up on Long Island, Scott Ialacci—alias MTV's DJ Skribble—didn't always have the full support of his family when it came to DJing. "My music got so loud that I had to move everything out into the garage. If I played too loud out there, my father would cut the power. I was out there every day after school, practicing for hours in the middle of January and February with a kerosene heater."

Skribble staved off frostbite and joined the rap outfit Young Black Teenagers in 1988; he also found time to spin with Primus and Anthrax during the Teenagers' four-year run, and he demonstrated tricks on *Showtime at the Apollo.* In between 1992 and 1997, he performed with acts like Craig Mack and Channel Live and even opened for The Chemical Brothers.

In 1996, he teamed with comedian Bill Irwin for the Broadway musical *Hip-Hop Wonderland.* "That was a big accomplishment. It wasn't kids coming to see that show. It was middle-aged people, from white, Middle America, seeing this stuff for the first time."

Now millions of ordinary Americans witness him in action regularly; he's seen three times daily as cohost of the weekly *MTV Jams.* Prior to making the jump to TV land, Skribble spent two years at New York radio's WQHT-FM, "Hot 97." As the man behind the hip-hop grooves of *Traffic Jams,* he helped make *Ed Love & Dr. Dre Mornings* a number-one morning show, while his own *Saturday Night After Party* kept dance jams pumping into the wee small hours.

Skribble continues to move between the two genres today, promoting hip-hop on his *Traffic Jams,* mixed CDs and house (with partner Anthony Acid) on the *MDMA* compilation. "Most hip-hop DJs can't play house, and most house DJs can't play hip-hop. I want to be the first DJ to live in both worlds successfully."

Tonight is your first DJ booking on unfamiliar turf, playing for a crowd you've never encountered before. Wanting everything to go smoothly, you plan out your entire set down to the last detail. All the bugs have been worked out of the tougher mixes, and you've filed the tunes in your crate in playback order. You hit the decks and get off to a smashing start, only to lay an egg about halfway through and lose three quarters of your dance floor. After waiting endlessly to mix into the next tune, the remaining dancers respond with lifeless shuffling, like extras in a zombie flick. In a matter of minutes, you've gone from walking on the clouds to stomping around in cement espadrilles. What happened? And how can you extricate yourself from the mess you've made?

Being married to a preordained program short-circuits the DJ's only feedback mechanism: interaction with the crowd. If they like what's spinning, that's fantastic. But if they don't, you're stuck playing tunes—however flawlessly—that aren't entertaining people. At that point, the club owner might as well just pop in a mix CD of popular tracks and send you packing. It's important to know which tunes work well together, but impromptu programming is essential, too.

> At first I was so nervous that I would have my entire set planned out ahead of time, record for record. If anyone looked through my records, I'd be flipping out. "Leave 'em in the order!" But when you think like that, the crowd is completely out of the picture. I started realizing, *Wow, there were times in my set where there wasn't as much energy.* Mixing from the heart and reading what they want to hear next is much more fun. I've got to please other people before I please myself.
>
> —DJ Tron

> Some people know what records they're going to play [beforehand], but I'd rather not be like that. Maybe you're playing after a DJ who's played all those records already. I'll go in and check

out the vibe of the party and go off the vibe that's been generated already.

—Jumping Jack Frost

I'm notorious among all the friends, because I bring everything. I'll bring six crates of records for a two-hour gig. I never want to get caught with my pants down—"I should have brought this record!" If you pigeonhole yourself and bring too much of one thing and don't bring some other stuff, then you're stuck.

—DJ Skribble

Naturally, if you're a big draw, you can be a little less flexible. . . .

We always have an idea of what we're going to play. It's always a "You're coming with us or you're going home" kind of thing. People have to make that leap of faith. And they'll be rewarded.

—Tom Rowlands (Chemical Brothers)

When you hire me, it's like you're hiring Patti LaBelle. She'll throw in some surprises, but basically you know what you're gonna get: one hell of a show. Yeah, you're going to hear the same songs, but you *love* those songs, so they're going to make you feel good. I throw some new things in here and there, but it has to fit the format.

—Jesse Saunders

Taking programming cues from the audience can be particularly tough when the DJ has certain tracks he or she is determined to make everyone else love, too. I felt like I was chopping off a digit when I stopped toting Loose Joints' "Tell You Today" to every gig. But I was just losing a sixth finger, because crowds never went nuts for it, and no amount of repeat spins made a difference.

Sometimes DJs want to expose a crowd to something that they love so badly it can be heartbreaking. But slowly but surely, you come to the reality that they're not going to respond the way you hope they will. And if you want to keep yourself employed, you have to react accordingly.

—Robbie Leslie

To this day, I still don't understand why if I like something and think it's amazing, other people don't.

—Ben Dubuisson (Purple Penguin)

Although building a groove and creating a mood is one important aspect of a set, never underestimate the capacity for abrupt transitions to keep people on their toes.

I practice improvisation in the set. I'll bring two or three times more records [than I can play], and I always bring surprise records, something that will make it a challenge. I don't mark my records, or bring the same records every set. If two white labels just came, I want to play them tonight.

—DJ Soul Slinger

It's really important to make tempo changes in a certain amount of time, like maybe two minutes. A radical tempo change, not just doing something at half speed, so people are really surprised, going, "What's going on now?" They are constantly aware of what they are listening to, so it never becomes the background.

—Alec Empire

Very often, I'll play something like Jimi Hendrix or a Beatles track, or a cheesy band from the '70s doing "Whole Lotta Love" that I picked up in a junk shop. That doesn't sound that original, but in a hip-hop club, some people go for it and some don't. You might lose a bit of the floor, but the people who really appreciate that are ones who are into the music.

—Scott Hendy (Purple Penguin)

I like buggin' people out with the things that I play, stuff that's kind of weird, but that at the same time people can get to it. I play a lot of songs that people haven't heard in a while, or somebody's first record. But I'm really selective. I'm about rocking the crowd and making people dance—*and* making them go, "Ooh . . . ."

—Prince Paul

A DJ has an advantage over a band, because he [or she] can make radical changes in a very short amount of time. When a band plays, they have a set and play certain songs. They can't really change [gears] and play some weird records from Russia.

—Alec Empire

Sometimes the most surprising thing a DJ can do is spin a superlative tune more than once. Usually a DJ will do this over the course of a whole evening, but that's not always the case. The night he debuted Skipworth & Turner's "Thinking About Your Love," Larry Levan purportedly let the Paradise Garage crowd hear it from start to finish over half a dozen times, until the crowd was going insane (that's a good thing). He'd simply play the whole song, pick up the needle as it slid into the out groove, and then drop it right back at the beginning.

There's a real influential club in Bristol called the Dugout, where Massive Attack used to play when they were [still called] the Wild Bunch. They were playing there when Soul II Soul first came out, and someone—I think it was Nellee Hooper—had an advance copy that week. And he slung it on and literally played it four times, and everyone was havin' it. That was a legendary moment in Bristol.

—Scott Hendy (Purple Penguin)

All of us know a good record when we hear it. If you're nuts about a record, you just play it...four or five times a night. I was the first person to play Mighty Clouds of Joy, and I played [that record] to death, because it was a fantastic record.
                                                    —Steve D'Acquisto

For aspiring DJs weaned on a diet of genre-specific programs (all house, all techno, all hip-hop), mixing records from different eras and musical styles coherently probably seems daunting. But when you boil music down to its elemental components—melody, harmony, timbre, tempo—it proves easier than one might imagine.

You always have a constant beat that will go through any music. If you can find that, it will all go together, if you understand music.
                                                    —Anita Sarko

House comes from a soulful, R&B-gospel-based background, and, of course, disco. That's the foundation. But the elements on top can be anything, from classical to new wave to rock. If you understand the roots of house, it's not far-fetched to relate it to [other things]. Musically, we're only dealing with twelve notes. Somewhere down the line, certain things are going to sound similar, even if they seem to be out in left field.
                                                    —Jesse Saunders

One programming consideration neophyte DJs don't always grasp immediately is using vocal tracks with lyrics as a means of creating a narrative within a set. Grouping songs by themes or in ways that suggest an unfolding story often proves more entertaining and inspiring then just hooking up songs by bpm or genre alone. One of my favorite minisets begins with a remix by the Grid of a tune by Boy George's Jesus Loves You project, followed by a Fatboy Slim big beat track, wrapping up with a 1985 single by gospel signer Tramaine Hawkins. Sound messy? Not when you realize all three—"Bow Down Mister," "Praise You," and "In the Morning"—offer up thanks to a higher power.

> I try to do things with words, with a story line, which seems to present itself if you listen. And playing not only from my head, but from my heart. Ultimately, the music is playing you.
>
> —David Mancuso

> We would take [lyrical] themes: Found My Man, Love My Man, Lost My Man, Got Him Again, He's a Fuck, and Now I'm Gonna Kick His Ass out that Door . . . and then, But I'd Take Him Back in a Heartbeat. Love and emotion had a lot to do with everything we did, and every way we did it.
>
> —Steve D'Acquisto

> When I DJ, there is a very definite sense of progressing through a story in the music, and that story evolves. The songs are together because that's what I want to do, not merely because they're the hot tracks of the moment or share ludicrously similar beats. There's actually a deep, heartfelt essence that comes out of the music. I'm always striving to figure out a way to play records that will convey those various essences, whether through the lyrics or [through] the mood of the music.
>
> —François K.

Disco innovator Walter Gibbons once observed, "There are spirits in the records. You really have to think that every time you change the record, the title or something about the record is going into people's heads." If a club or party DJ is doing his or her job well, the people dancing probably aren't scrutinizing the actual meanings behind the words they're hearing, even though they may be singing along. Since a savvy programmer can use this for positive—or negative—effect, some argue that DJs must be sensitive to the social repercussions of such a transfer.

> Depending on how you present music to the crowd, that's how you're going to influence what they dance to, what they like, and so forth. I don't think a lot of DJs really understand that responsibility. It's like listening to the radio. They play all this gangsta [rap] craziness and then don't understand why people are in gangs and shooting each other!
>
> —Jesse Saunders

> There's a danger that when lyrics are used in a very negative sense, it can be really taken to extremes. But I don't feel that it is my duty or obligation to play anyone's music that refers to that. Because those things are not just lyrics, they're reality. They promote the reality of people getting shot, the reality of hate, and they become the reality of bigotry and discrimination.
>
> —François K.

Ever scratch your head and wonder just what DJs mean when they say the music they're spinning is "old school"? A survey of our experts suggests that they're referring to a more diverse programming approach, and not necessarily the term's implied definition of confining the selections within specific chronological boundaries.

> My crossover can be anything from the Orb to Van Morrison to Crown Heights Affair. Basically, my roots are in jazz, but I do get into a very heavy dance vibe. I pick records by following the sonic trail in the vibrations.
>
> —David Mancuso

> There was really nothing we wouldn't play in the old days. We played slow music, too. You had to, so people would go and

drink. I was the first person to play Carole King's "It's Too Late." The bouncer wanted to kill me.

—Steve D'Acquisto

What was cool was back then was you could play a larger variety of beats. You went from one extreme to the next. Now everything's in synch, just so you can dance to it.

—Prince Paul

I like mixing up all types of music. I came up from a generation where everyone mixed with everyone, no prejudices. In the old days, Mark Kamins at Danceteria would go from Konk to T-La Rock's "It's Yours," and people would just be going crazy. DJs can't do that today. And if they do, they're looked at like "What the fuck did you just do?"

—Kurtis Mantronik

When you think about all the types of music we played, it was pretty amazing. You exposed different people to different music. The rock and rollers got introduced to James Brown, and the Motown folks got into rock and roll, and everybody lived a full, happy, musical life. Now you go to a club and you don't know where it starts and ends. If I were playing now, I would play the Foo Fighters and Everclear and Tool and Bush, all kinds of things with amazing beats. And that would be just my rock and roll part of the night.

—Steve D'Acquisto

The content of the music has changed dramatically [since I started], but my style hasn't. Even though the tempo of music is more restrictive lately—there really is no music in the range between one hundred and one hundred sixteen bpm, or above one hundred thirty-six—I still start out easy. Even if it's not down tempo, it's more passive music for setting the scene. You can still be very creative with songs the majority of people are familiar with and like. It doesn't have to be tired; it doesn't mean Madonna and Gloria Estefan in this day, or Miguel Brown and Evelyn "Champagne" King back at the Saint. I apply old rules to new music. That's why I consider myself old school.

—Robbie Leslie

Disco and hip-hop aren't the only musical movements that incorporated a wide array of musical styles under one gigantic umbrella. Although scenes that emerged later, like house and techno, often seem to be defined, even constricted, by very narrow aesthetics, their roots are surprisingly expansive.

I grew up on rock and everything else, so I didn't stick to disco like "Let No Man Put Asunder." I got tired of playing that after six or seven years. It was nice to drop in now and then, but a lot of people wanted to hear that stuff all the time. I played rock, funk, R&B, disco, and everything from the Go-Go's and Devo to the B-52's' "Mesopotamia."

—Jesse Saunders

When I was first starting to play records, it was an eclectic mix, from Front 242 and Nitzer Ebb to "Jack Your Body" and Derrick May tracks. Even Derrick [May] and Jeff [Mills] played that on their mix shows and when they were playing out. That was the sound of Detroit at the time.

—Richie Hawtin (Plastikman)

In the late '80s, in Ibiza's Balearic scene, DJs like Alfredo would throw anything from UK indie pop by the Woodentops to flamenco music to Blondie's "Atomic" into the mix. When Paul Oakenfold imported the sound to England and launched Spectrum at Heaven, the same eclectic sensibility—anything that keeps the punters dancing—prevailed. Even at the expense of fluid mixing.

> The Balearic scene was about playing the best of collected music together. You heard LL Cool J mixed into Nirvana, into Bob Marley and then a house record. Because I'd grown up on pop music, that really appealed to me. I took that sound, spirit, and energy of the island, which was "Let's go and have a party and enjoy ourselves, rather than standing with a long face at the bar." Musically, what I was mixing, the collection of sounds was all over the shop tempo-wise. It was really hard to mix it all together . . . and sometimes it didn't work.
>
> —Paul Oakenfold

Although the practice isn't as common as it was in the '70s, today there are still plenty of contemporary DJs who cover a lot of musical terrain in the course of a set and are willing to take chances.

> I grew up in D.C. The Bad Brains are in my blood. I've worked with Xenakis, I plan to remix some John Cage material, and Philip Glass and [I] have been talking forever about doing a project. Meanwhile, I just remixed Korn's last single as a big beat track. I like ambient, hip-hop, and drum and bass. It's all just different sides of the same coin.
>
> DJ Spooky

> We're not the kind of DJs who are getting sent a lot of records and change the records we play every week. We find more obscure records and turn them into classics for us. We make something that doesn't appear to be a dance floor record into a dance-floor record.
>
> —Tom Rowlands (Chemical Brothers)

And yet, there are DJs and dancers alike who trumpet the merits of one stripe of music over all others. That's perfectly valid, but in many cases, a crash course in musical history might open up their eyes. One afternoon in the late '80s, a DJ friend ten years my senior planted my singularly synth-pop sensibility down on the sofa and told me to shut up and listen. He started slapping on Pet Shop Boys and Giorgio Moroder and Kraftwerk tracks without letting me know which was what and defied me to clearly distinguish why some tracks sounded "better" than others. Without the benefit of seeing the bands' haircuts, I couldn't do it. It's a phase many of us go through.

> Young DJs don't understand [diversity] as much. They seemed to be locked into one groove and become purists: drum and bass, hip-hop, techno, or house.
>
> —Barry Ashworth

> People like to identify with a particular group of people. To say "I am a...whatever" gives them security. You get fascists in England, hip-hop fascists and such. They don't understand that some of their idols were actually mixing it up. Lots of classic hip-hop tracks wouldn't have been made if the people starting off the scene hadn't been listening to New Order or Kraftwerk.
>
> —Ben Dubuisson (Purple Penguin)

> If you like hip-hop, you've got to like rock, funk, and soul, because all that other music makes up your hip-hop. If kids were to sit there and ask, "Where'd you get that beat from?" they would be surprised when some of these DJs told them.
>
> —Afrika Bambaataa

> People have lost their imagination on a lot of fronts. They feel they have to cling to whatever little style name—tech-step, drum and bass, two-step, terror-step, hard house, trance. My

philosophy is a bit more inclusive. I'm open. But when people encounter that [attitude], they're like, "This guy's pulling the rug out from under all our little boundaries."

—DJ Spooky

Even polished pros who've made their reputations championing a single genre realize there's always room for diversity within a set, even if that just means pushing the envelope within that isolated scene.

We have a bit of every kind of drum and bass in our set. We can't play a whole set of one style, because we just love everything. We're narrow-minded purists about drum and bass—we don't really listen to any other kind of music—but we love every part of drum and bass.

—Storm (Kemistry & Storm)

To this day, when I hear kids in record stores or at parties talking about their passion for one very specific subgenre of music, I get uptight. Perhaps I'm just embarrassed, remembering my own adolescent tunnel vision, but when you step back from the picture, you can see why diehard purists are an essential part of the musical landscape.

When a kid talks only about German trance, why is that? Because in his little universe, as all the musical multicolors are unfolding, he's one little pattern on the DNA [of dance music]. Because of his perspective, that music is everything. He's playing [tunes released on] those ten labels from Germany that make those ten clubs in that scene, those people banging on ecstasy. And if you see that in a bigger picture of the whole helix, then [his narrow scope] doesn't matter.

—DJ Soul Slinger

The majority of people have their specific focus, and that's what they want to deal with. And then there's a few weirdos pushing the envelope a little bit harder, which usually turns up some interesting stuff. Which in due course will filter over into the mainstream and get diluted and commercialized, just leaving the way free for more mad shit to come up. That's an eternal cycle.

—Matt Black (Coldcut)

Ultimately, whether a DJ is working exclusively with hard trance twelve-inches made in Frankfurt, or a spectrum encompassing everything from wax cylinders of Wagner to drum and bass DATs, the truest measure of a DJ's programming skills hinges on the effectiveness of the selections in communicating with a specific crowd. But that's the next chapter.

There is no way that you can ever call someone a good or bad DJ. Just like you can never call someone a good or bad painter. If you look at a picture of a puppy dog with big eyes, painted in a yellow that matches your yellow couch, and go, "That's exactly the painting I'm looking for. . . . Isn't that a cute puppy?" that is a great painting—for you. The same person might look at a painting of a puppy dog with its nose on the side of its head, painted in puce, and go, "What the fuck is that?" But then you'll get an avant-garde person going "That's genius!"

—Anita Sarko

8 The Good, the Bad, and the Ugly

I like the psychology of being a DJ, knowing I can control people without [their] knowing it.

—Prince Paul

If the previous two chapters were about the technical (mixing) and aesthetic (programming) nuts and bolts of a being a DJ, think of this one as addressing the psychological and spiritual aspects of the craft. Calling what a DJ does spiritual might strike those of little faith as New Age babble, but if you've ever experienced a truly phenomenal DJ set—from either side of the decks—it's an idea a hell of a lot easier to swallow than color-coordinating your chakras.

Regardless of the venue or what kind of music a DJ is spinning, developing a rapport with the audience is essential for a successful gig. For a big-name jock like Junior Vasquez or Funkmaster Flex, this isn't as daunting. Those guys have established reputations, and people come with very clear expectations of what they're going to hear.

Junior Vasquez is my biggest inspiration, as far as house music goes. He has such control over his crowd every week. He's the only after-hours DJ that I know who keeps people there until six o'clock the next night. When you walk into that place, you're walking into his movie, and you're a character. There are so many different characters in that club and they all play an intricate part in his little world and how he plays records.

—DJ Skribble

But most DJs don't have such a dedicated base of operations, so even before the music starts playing, they need to try to hook up with the vibe of the crowd. If that sounds like being a mind reader, to a degree it is—and even some of the biggest DJs in the world aren't entirely sure how they figure out what people want to hear.

It's really important that there's a link between the people and the DJ. I just see myself as an instrument of the crowd. I feel the crowd giving me their energy and demanding certain things from me, and I just bounce their energy back to them, amplified, through the music. It's not because of me that the party's going to go crazy. It's because of them. Without those people, there would just be one DJ playing in a room, bullshitting. Those people in the room are the most important thing.

—François K.

In Miami recently, I played behind DJ Hurricane. It was Sunday, normally a hip-hop night for this club. They'd have been mad if I'd come straight on. But he ran down the top twenty hip-hop tracks, which satisfied them and got them all loose. Cool, perfect. When I came on, I didn't go against the grain. A hip-hop crowd will go for house tracks, if they're soulful and funky enough. I started in with some nice, New York disco-house tracks, then got into my thing gradually. At the end of my set, all those same people that were there for the hip-hop were still around. That was a good feeling.

—Juan Atkins

You aren't home making a tape for your own gratification. You're working for an establishment, and it's your job to satisfy and make a lot of people happy. And if you're going to do it with the music that you like, you have to do it with music they want to hear as well.

—Peter Calandra

If you go into a club and it's not an underground or after-hours club but you play like you would in one of those places, the kids are going to look at you like you're nuts, and they're not going to enjoy themselves. I've got to play a record that's going to make the kids dance. It's not for me. It's for them. I get my enjoyment from watching them scream when I throw in a record they like. There's a way to sprinkle that [underground music] in with what they like, and then they'll appreciate it more.

—DJ Skribble

My pitch is good, my rhythm is good, and if it mixes, I'm going to mix it. But I don't always know what's gonna rock the crowd. That's more Jon's side of things. I'm usually pretty petrified if I have to rock a dance floor, although I've done it many times. Jon gets petrified as well, but he doesn't show it as much as I do.

—Matt Black (Coldcut)

How that link is created is a two-step process. Before the music even begins, a savvy mixmaster will do detective work: What is the crowd like, in terms of age, background, and general character? What is the overall ambience of the venue? Look at the room you're playing in, and incorporate that into programming decisions, too.

And then, once the music starts pumping, DJs have actual feedback from the assembled to tell them how they're doing. Acknowledging the crowd doesn't have to stop with record selections, either—great DJs are often dancing along behind the turntables, clapping in rhythm, banging on percussion instruments, and shouting out loud. And not just because they're fanning the flames. They're part of a circuit with the crowd and are having a good time right along with them.

> Some DJs are intimidated by crowds. What they don't realize is that they're people just like you. When I get up there, I think like I'm one of the people in the crowd: *How am I going to be affected? What do I want to hear?*
>
> —Juan Atkins

> It's almost like you're a medium for everyone in the party. That's something I learned a long time ago. You put it all together and feed it back to the people. But mastering the translation between you and the crowd is something you have to work on.
>
> —Jumping Jack Frost

> The more you DJ, the more you can read your crowd and the better you get. That's something that becomes stronger and stronger the longer that you DJ.
>
> —Heather Heart

> For Larry Levan, or David Mancuso, or Nicky Siano—these people who started the early New York movement—there was always this element of being in the crowd, the feeling that through the record, the DJ was speaking directly to you. I question whether DJs that are just coming up now understand that [dynamic] or are aware that it actually exists and takes place. I'm after that cathartic experience where you feel that it changes your life.
>
> —François K.

> When I go into a room, the first thing that talks to me is the room itself. What kind of room is it? If there is a bar, where is it situated in reference to the dance floor? How big is the dance

floor? What kind of lighting and sound system is there? People are affected by the environment they're in. If you have a certain feeling in a room, you can almost imagine that everyone in there is going to have a similar feeling.

—Juan Atkins

You can't stand behind the decks, head lowered, just moving your hands, ignoring the audience. I'm always running around and jumping about, shouting and dancing. In my band, I'm the front man, the center of attention. It's the same position when you DJ—you're a performer. That's why I'm very animated.

—Barry Ashworth

Return engagements and steady residencies affords DJs a chance to forge even stronger bonds with their crowd. Conversely, accepting opportunities to play engagements outside of their usual milieu sharpens skills by allowing them to learn how to entertain a broader range of people. And if you know what you're getting into ahead of time, you can plan accordingly—even if planning means not taking a job.

When I was at my peak in New York, I used to work at a straight joint called the Red Parrot, a club called Underground, and the Saint. I liked that challenge of playing to different demographics, because DJing is all about hooking up with the soul of your crowd. It's not about forcing them to like what you want them to, and it's not my-way-or-the-highway.

—Robbie Leslie

We've got such an idiosyncratic way of playing. We go play techno clubs in the north of England, but people still understand why we're playing in there. That's one thing we're quite good at: We can play different places.

—Tom Rowlands (Chemical Brothers)

We're quite careful about where we play. We like a level of anticipation and excitement. Our set is very demanding. We don't just play a smooth house mix for the few kids still wanting to have it on a Sunday night. If we're playing Glastonbury [a big UK music festival] on a Friday, that's a dream booking, whereas maybe a small club in the middle of Manhattan is not necessarily right for us.

—Ed Simons (Chemical Brothers)

People would always say, "You never played the big rooms." After the first few weeks at Palladium, they wanted me to play the main floor. But I didn't want to, because then you couldn't be creative. It was like playing a shopping mall in New Jersey.

—Anita Sarko

[Back in the Bronx] you had to know what part of the audience you were playing your jams for. One minute you might be playing for the hustle people, and the next you might be playing for the b-boys and b-girls who'd be tearing the floor up . . . next thing, you're playing for everybody to get crazy.

—Afrika Bambaataa

The Mudd Club was basically a group of reactionaries. If you had to have [the vibe] explained to you, then you didn't understand it. I was always dodging glasses and ashtrays, because the stuff I played would anger people so much they'd throw things. But I had this group of people who would come in at three in the morning, like Jean-Michel Basquiat and Vincent Gallo, and they just loved [the music]. The people earlier on in the night couldn't understand why I'd be playing Public Image Ltd. next to Funkadelic. They didn't see the connection.

—Anita Sarko

I used to work at a Bristol club called Misty's, which was pretty terrible. For the first hour and a half, I played whatever I wanted, great rap and disco records. Then everybody would start coming in, and I had to play Top 40. Many people probably wouldn't admit working in a club playing Madonna and Fine Young Cannibals, but learning to please people, or how to deal with people coming up and giving you a hassle, was invaluable. A lot of DJs would want to go straight from their bedrooms into a big club, playing all the latest sounds, without ever doing any of that. But that's why they [experience] a bit of a shock sometimes.

—Andy Smith

Considering the many benefits of having a captive audience that appreciates an individual programming style, it's no wonder certain jocks make an extra effort to throw their own events, concerning themselves with details far beyond the music and their drink ticket allotment. For patrons of clubs like Paradise Garage, the Loft, NASA, or Body & Soul, going to hear the DJs synonymous with those places almost approximates a pilgrimage. And with that kind of participation and love from the crowd, the DJ has a much better shot at providing them with a religious experience.

A party is a very important thing. It's an opportunity for people to congregate, make friends, and forge bonds. That opportunity is rare in the normal context of our modern city life. People talk about how important integration is, but very few people are trying to do anything about it. Part of our philosophy is based on not discriminating against anyone. We just want to provide a safe, comfortable environment where you can do whatever you like with the music, dance and celebrate and enjoy.

—François K.

"If you've got a regular crowd that you play to every week, you can take them on a much deeper journey. If it's for a long period of time, I'm happier playing to two hundred people rather than two thousand. You can take more chances and play stuff that you wouldn't necessarily play if you've only got an hour at a big rave.

—DJ DB

We're lucky that we have our own scene that we were able to create, without other people—who are better at ordering cases of Heineken and finding out who's on the coat check—telling the DJ what to play. Body & Soul should be an encouragement for anyone out there to start their own scenes, however small, and to persevere. That's the only way that they're going to find meaningful growth.

—François K.

The bottom line in many cases, though, is that DJs are on some-body's payroll. And if they aren't doing their job to the satisfaction of whoever is signing their check (or more likely, passing them a folded wad of bills after last call), that jock will soon be looking for a new place to play. Unfortunately, this can often have an adverse influence on a DJ's programming—why risk being on food stamps when simply running down the *Billboard* Top 20 Hot Dance singles will surely please?

Because then you're just a glorified jukebox, surrendering part of your originality to the mundane mandates of the mainstream record business. Plus, you're making it easier for someone else to distinguish him- or herself with truly inspired selections and perhaps land the next gig instead of you. Any DJ who finds a club owner, promoter, or other patron of the turntable arts with whom he or she feels a con-nection is wise to nurture that relationship; working for people who defer to your aesthetic is a rare luxury!

Every job is different. It's a matter of adapting to the particular policies of the organization. Some are very amenable, and management will give you artistic license. And at some, you leave at the end of the night wanting to retire altogether.

—Robbie Leslie

If you're dealing with club owners and the pressures of getting gigs instead of other people [getting them], that puts you in the same kind of stance as TV networks going after ratings. Everyone becomes bland and very similar, because they're all competing on a very narrow ground.

—François K.

In light of all the different factors that influence any gig—the venue, the people, the musical trends of the day—I made sure to ask the DJs I interviewed what their favorite types of places to play were—and why. Specific elements found within special audiences—a degree of physical and psychological intimacy, enthusiastic feedback, a willingness to be open to new experiences—were mentioned time and again.

People have cried when I play. "Man, this means so much." That's really intense. Sometimes I don't know what to say to them. I've had the opposite, too. People have wanted to kill me. But the reactions are always extreme, which I see as positive.

—Alec Empire

Most young DJs have never witnessed that time of the party where the energy gets so intense that everybody starts screaming and hollering. That is what I'm striving for, to provide them with the backdrop to actually feel comfortable and stimulated enough that they go to the point of no return, like a sort of a musical orgasm.

—François K.

I played this one little hardcore show in Denver, in this old punk rock club. There were maybe a hundred people there, but it was so cool. The sound was pounding in this small place, and everybody knew each other. There was no attitude, and everyone was bouncing. That's a much better environment, and much more fun, too, than if you're placed way above eight thousand people.

—DJ Tron

I like smaller parties, where everybody either knows each other, or will get to know everybody during the night. An amalgamation of sounds, different styles segmented together properly over the night, is really key. And it's important for the people to be really open, loving, spiritual people. You can always feel that in a room, as soon as you walk in, if it is or it isn't there. And people should dance when they go to these parties. If everybody's dancing, that's very special.

—Heather Heart

On the other hand, for everything that can go right at an engagement, there are also a million things that can go wrong. Drop one bum tune and the next thing you know you're wiping an enraged patron's rum and Coke off your face. Realizing that rotten gigs make for great anecdotes (comedy = tragedy + timing), here are the tales of some of our participants' worst and weirdest DJing experiences. These should clear up any confusion about why knowing who you're playing for beforehand is always useful information.

I was DJing a show in Berlin, and twenty security people came up and said I had to stop because the energy was getting too aggressive. "What do you mean?" I said. "I'm the headliner." I stopped the record, and the kids were freaking out. I started just repeating samples, this hip-hop a cappella saying, "Suck my dick." These security people wanted to beat me up, and the kids started throwing bottles at them. When it ended, I [played] two noise records and pushed the faders up to the top. The noise was destroying the whole PA. I left without getting paid.

—Alec Empire

My first club gig was with Dr. Dre, Chuck D, and MC Flava Flav—before Public Enemy—Doug E. Fresh, and LL Cool J. My sister knew the guys, so they let me play, and I was the worst. Horrible! Here I am, this little white boy in an all-black club, and they're looking at me like "What are you doing?"

—DJ Skribble

After NASA closed, I was so sick of kiddie ravers—and their bullshit drugs and bullshit fashion—that I went completely the opposite direction and did a party called Trash. Initially, we got a very trendy, slightly older, English crowd. I was playing "trash" music, everything from Fleetwood Mac, Lynyrd Skynyrd, and the Cranberries to Donna Summer, Nirvana, and Divine. It started as a sick joke, but the English people quickly got bored. What we were left with was a Long Island crowd who thought it was the best club ever. We were sold out every night. By the end of three months, I hated the crowd and those records. But it was incredible to have a roomful of kids pogo-ing to Nirvana.

 DJ DB

Once I was doing a show with John Lydon [aka Johnny Rotten]. The audience was punk, and I threw on Led Zeppelin. Boy, they cussed me and booed me. I said, "Let me tell you something—don't even act like you don't like Led Zeppelin. All y'all were into this shit before you got into punk!"

—Afrika Bambaataa

I had one gig where the first DJ didn't show up, so the promoter told me to start playing. The DJ booth was an aluminum tower that was very wobbly and I was about thirty feet up. Of course, the first DJ turned up thirty minutes late, finds that he's lost his set, and then starts shaking the tower violently every time I try to mix two records.

—Mixmaster Morris

One of the weirdest places I've ever played was a nuclear bomb shelter in St. Petersburg, Russia. There was this sense of brooding violence. While I was DJing, the Russian secret service showed up. A lot of Russians [were] taking currency and switching it to American and leaving the country with it. The nightclubs are where people launder money. That was so strange, because I was an African-American amidst this bugged-out white Russian vibe. You want to talk about feeling alienated? But I was shocking to them. These guys with machine guns, in army camouflage, coming down the stairs into a club in their own city . . . and seeing a black guy with green dreadlocks spinning really twisted jungle records.

DJ Spooky

I once got booked for an army officers' function, in a hall full of portraits of generals. The location was a secret for security reasons. It wasn't a success! I once got hired to play in Majorca (the poor man's Ibiza) alongside Black Box and C+C Music Factory. I once played in Japan under a sun so strong all my records just melted in the heat. I once flew to Sardinia to find my records hadn't made it. And once I flew to L.A. for a New Year's Eve party that the police closed down before it started.

—Mixmaster Morris

I was playing in Manila, at an outside free party, organized by the Goethe Institute. They were passing it off as a German culture [event], and it was seen as a very hip thing. A lot of rich Filipino people came down, but because it was free, there were also lots of street kids. I had to stop after twenty minutes; the police came and pulled the plug. There were shots [fired]. It was really confrontational, which is exactly what this music is about. That was the most intense show I ever did . . . so far.

—Alec Empire

But sometimes, despite the best of intentions, the DJ finds the odds just aren't stacked in his or her favor.

We DJ and we play live. That's a very basic distinction, but people still find it very confusing. "We thought you were playing live, but you're just playing records."

—Tom Rowlands (Chemical Brothers)

But when we play live, people think, *Oh, it's just a couple of DJs. Oh, you wanted us to be boring . . . but not that way. You wanted us to be boring the other way!*

—Ed Simons (Chemical Brothers)

Recently, I made a mistake [at a gig] *I went, I'm gonna do this old school,* so the last record I put on was a slow jam. Guys find a girl, and girls find a guy, and everybody gets on the floor. It was a classic—"Always and Forever" by Heatwave—and it didn't work. The crowd looked at me like I was dumb, and everybody went to the wall.

—Prince Paul

In a perfect world, hard-working DJs would never have to contend with undue interference from audience members. But even if jocks restrict bookings to church functions and bar mitzvahs, inevitably they'll run into a civilian who knows how to do their job better than they do and is hell-bent on making that little fact widely known. Most events that feature DJs typically entail alcohol or other mood-altering substances, which make the user—but not the DJ—invulnerable to criticism.

Take my own sorry example. One night at my drag-show residency, I had a drunken patron come up and start staring at me. I ignored him for a minute, pretending to be lost in the mix. He began berating me loudly in front of the crowd, for both my selections and my failure to beat match—as if beat-matching Amon Tobin's bossa nova drum and bass and Henry Mancini's Latin brass rendition of "Springtime for Hitler" was a no-brainer. I just smirked and started rummaging in my box. The night was almost over, and I didn't need a hassle.

Next thing I know, I hear an enormous crash of breaking glass. My disgruntled detractor had backhanded the lava lamp I had erected next to the decks (that's what I get for trying to achieve added ambience on my own dime), sending shards flying all over the room. There was now a huge pool of hot oil for customers to navigate as they tried to exit the dance floor. I leaped out from behind the DJ station, grabbed Miss Thing by the arm, and starting screaming obscenities in this twerp's face until a bouncer arrived to escort him out.

I felt proud of myself until after we'd locked up and the bartenders informed me that my fearsome display had actually sounded like a top-notch hissy fit to anyone who hadn't witnessed the earlier proceedings. In the interests of preserving what shreds of masculinity I've managed to accrue over the years, I now let other people—bouncers, friends at hand—run interference in such situations and try to maintain concentration on the music. And I leave my lava lamp at home.

I hit someone once while I was playing. There was a group of about ten people in front of me who were friends with this other DJ, and they just really wanted him to go on. I could see them going [mimes jerking off] "wanker" out of the corner of my eye. Finally I snapped.

I jumped over the decks and smacked about three of them; the rest ran. I made the jump back and put the next record on before it ran out. The crowd saw what I'd done, and the place was cheering. Then the promoter came up and said, "I've got to put on the other DJ." I said, "There's no fuckin' way that guy's getting on the decks now!" But I don't generally go whacking punters.

—Barry Ashworth

I've been to places where my crew will perform for a crowd that doesn't necessarily care how well we can scratch, or that we're four DJs with four turntables all jamming at the same time. All they want to hear is Mase and Puffy. Promoters book you thinking, *Damn, I love these guys, so they must like 'em, too.* Then when the crowd sees us and realizes that what we're doing is more turntablism, you'll hear, "Oh, can we hear some music now?" But you just keep playing, because there are interested people in that crowd who want to hear what you do.

—Rob Swift

The most hostile thing someone can do at a dance club is leave the floor, and that happens to me. I thought a song was gonna be perfect, [but] the dance floor clears. Often that's because the song is drastically different from the one before; I've gotten in trouble with sets because I like so many different styles. But a lot of times, people leave, and then they start getting into the song, and by the middle or end they're all back there.

—Peanut Butter Wolf

Johnny [Dynell] used to kid me that I'd made my entire career out of driving people off of dance floors. But after a week, suddenly their foot would start tapping to a record. After two, their body would start moving. And after three weeks, they were on the dance floor.

—Anita Sarko

161

Discussions of hostility naturally segue into the touchy subject of taking requests. Whether you choose to honor them or not, aim to field them with grace. If you don't care to accept kibitzing from the peanut gallery, be prepared from strong responses from people who assume you're working exclusively for them. I had a drag queen faint on me once after she asked for Madonna's "Frozen" and I disclosed that I didn't have anything by the Material Girl handy.

My rule of thumb is if the request is something I've got, I'll work it in; if I've got something similar, I might suggest it as an alternative. A patron who's tuned into your programming taste deserves to be indulged. Especially if he's really cute and a little inebriated. Otherwise, just say, "No, I don't have that" as nicely as possible. Persistent suggestions should be met with a polite "I'm sorry, I don't take requests." As long as other folks seem to be having a good time (and assuming the venue has a functional metal detector at the door), then just keep on doing what you're doing.

Walter Gibbons used to say he happily took requests because he liked to know what his audience was thinking. If he didn't necessarily like the sentiment of what they'd chosen, he'd still try to honor it, then follow it with a track that featured a message he wanted to impart. (His classic example was pairing "Nasty Girl" with "Try God" by the New York Community Choir.) Here are some other opinions on how to handle this all-too-common predicament.

> The hostile people are guys who just want to hear a certain group. "Play some Wu-Tang Clan!" Now, I'm a big Wu-Tang fan, but maybe I didn't bring anything by them that night. But [the people are] drunk, and that's what they've got in their mind that they want to hear. If you don't have it, you're not a "good" DJ in their eyes.
>
> —Peanut Butter Wolf

It's important to listen to your crowd. If someone makes a request and I've got the record, I'll say, "Yeah, I'll play it." And I'll fit it in over the course of the night.

—Paul Oakenfold

I listen when people make requests. Parties can become very psychic. There will be moments where somebody will ask, "Can you play..." and you hit the [start] button and *boom!* You're looking at each other, because it's the record you were both thinking about. I've seen that happen many times.

—David Mancuso

I play in a lot of clubs that accept hip-hop primarily, but I play a really open set, which hopefully appeals to a lot of people. But, for example, when I'm playing that Peggy Lee cut "Sitting on the Dock of the Bay," some people will think, *Oh, he's playing a record I actually know.... That means I can ask for something else that I know.* And they'll come up and ask for ABBA.

—Andy Smith

We have had the odd occasion where maybe a person's gone to the wrong rave. At some places you'll be asked, "Is this the only music of the night? Can't you play anything else?" "Well, we don't want to. And the crowd doesn't want us to." We're always polite about those kind of things, though.

—Storm (Kemistry & Storm)

Over the years I've developed a list of snappy comebacks. Usually it's girls who'll come over going, "Haven't you got anything I can dance to?" I sort of take a step back and go... "Looking at you, I don't think so." Or, "Haven't you got anything good?" "Of course not. I don't actually have *anything* good."

—DJ DB

So you've learned how to mix records and program them in a refreshing, distinctive order. You hunt out sounds that should electrify listeners and you build relationships with people in positions to get or give you jobs. And yet, some DJs just can't seem to connect with the crowd. If this happens to you from time to time, just accept that everyone has a bad night and leave the self-flagellation to Henry Rollins and religious zealots.

If the situation persists and you still feel confident about your DJ technique, try to figure out what variable is missing from the equation to make it click while still being true to your own muse. And if, after all that, you're still playing to empty rooms or unreceptive audiences . . . well, nobody appreciated van Gogh in his lifetime, either.

> Everything influences me, and I learn things every day. That's why I feel like I'm never going to be a successful mainstream DJ. On one side, I represent and play for the people. And that's important. But on the other side, I want to show you what I learned I today. And [only] ten percent of the heads are going to get it, because they are on the same quest that I am. Which is not about just the appearance of things, but experiencing music. And music is a vast experience.
>
> —DJ Soul Slinger

> I definitely come with an agenda; I'm no jukebox. That sparks a weird warfare. My DJ sets have many facets; it depends on what environment I'm in. I have a piece called *Isotope* at an art gallery right now. I made these mixes of sound works from different [visual] artists—Andy Warhol, Joseph Beuys, Jean Dubuffet—with different contemporary music, everything from Cornelius to Talvin Singh, Steve Reich playing backward, and Public Enemy run through a weird echo chamber. I like being able to fluidly move between environments. Some of my programs are hyper-

experimental, verging on noise or chaos music, and others are straight-up dance sets. Whenever you're moving between zones, it leaves you open to attack. But so be it.

—DJ Spooky

There's a great Baudelaire piece about how it is not valid for an artist to blame the public for not liking one's art. Art is no more than communication, and the person who initiates the communication is the person upon whom the responsibility of it is placed. Nobody asked you to play music. So for you to go, "Peons, you don't get it!"—that may make you feel good, but it's not valid in art. You have to figure out, "How can I be true to myself as an artist who has decided to put my art out in the public domain and still make them go, 'Ah . . .'?" Now you may be one of those poor souls who isn't appreciated until you're dead. That doesn't mean [your art] isn't valid. Unfortunately, sometimes you are a person out of your own time. But if you have to cast blame, you have to share it. Or just feel secure within yourself.

—Anita Sarko

Sometimes you've got to wait another generation. You've got to wait in the desert for forty years, for the next generation to evolve and save the people. But eventually it happens.

—DJ Soul Slinger

9 All That Scratchin'

These days, when youngsters announce, "I want to be a DJ," they typically aspire to one of two ideals: (1) the globetrotting club jock, mixing epic sets for ecstatic dancers at packed clubs and raves, or (2) a turntablist. Turntablism, the art of the turntablist, promotes the record player as a tool for creating completely new music, not just playing prerecorded music. Working either in crews or as solo artists, today's turntablists, such as the X-ecutioners, Invisbl Skratch Piklz, Beat Junkies, Kid Koala, Peanut Butter Wolf, Cut Chemist, and Scratch Perverts, are among the most visible and influential DJs around.

> We're proving that this is not some type of novelty or gimmick. We're making albums and selling records now. Hopefully, in the years to come, the right people will understand how much of an art this is. You'll start to see it the way you see a person singing or rapping. It'll just be more accessible, not so underground.
>
> —Rob Swift

Turntablism is currently riding the crest of a swelling wave of media attention and widespread acceptance. Not only is the music distinctive, but this new school of DJs has brought a renewed visual flair to its gymnastic displays, making the behind-the-back cuts of Grandmaster Flash look like a beginner's yoga demonstration played back in slow motion.

> Ninety-nine percent of DJs, including myself, are not very interesting to look at. They put a record on, they mix in the next record, then take the record off. But Kid Koala is interesting to watch, because he works the turntables very hard.
> —Matt Black (Coldcut)

> The DJs today took things way beyond my imagination. That's why I know I can't be competitive anymore. I'd get wiped off the planet right about now.
> —Prince Paul

DJs like Q-Bert and Rob Swift are not only making innovative albums but also gaining national recognition. Mixmaster Mike's stint spinning for the Beastie Boys has exposed the DJ's magic to millions of mainstream consumers—and even spawned a Beasties tune ("Three MCs and One DJ").

> When you use that turntable as an instrument, you're a musician. That's why Mixmaster Mike was such a big part of the Beastie Boys tour. The Beasties didn't want to know what he was going to throw at them. They wanted to be surprised. The way he put the music together was amazing. He was the conductor of that whole show.
> —DJ Skribble

> One thing that made me really happy was I got to see the Beastie Boys perform on the MTV Music Awards, and we got to see [Mixmaster] Mike. They actually let Mike shine, scratching live on

camera. But I want to reach the point where you don't have to have the Beastie Boys and you could just see Mike up there.

—Rob Swift

The basic tenets of turntablism predate both hip-hop and disco by almost fifty years. Avant-garde composers John Cage and Pierre Schaeffer anticipated the evolution of the turntable as an independent instrument. In 1937, Cage suggested using four decks and customized recordings to create "a quartet for explosive motor, wind, heartbeat, and landslide." A decade later, Schaeffer created new compositions by isolating passages from existing recordings, then manipulating their sounds via turntable speed, volume, physical alteration of the grooves, and playing the wax backward.

Although with the advent of scratching in the late '70s turntablism was recontextualized as pop culture, it also evolved concurrently in more rarified circles than from whence it first sprung. During the '80s, when the status of the DJ in hip-hop was declining, New York artist Christian Marclay continued to advance concepts of turntablism in the art world, via installations and performance pieces that directly involved altering records or playback mechanisms.

As discussed in Chapter Three, Grandmaster Flash's 1982 opus "The Adventures of Grandmaster Flash on the Wheels of Steel" was the pioneering record to expose the art of the turntable to wider audiences. But the platter that truly brought the sound of cutting and scratching to the nation's ears and changed notions of what DJs did was Herbie Hancock's 1983 single "Rockit," one of two tunes from the jazz innovator's LP *Future Shock* to feature the talents of Zulu Nation DJ Grandmixer D.ST.

The song "Rockit" by Herbie Hancock was what really got me going. I remember that break—"Fr-fr-fr-fresshhh"—and I started scratching with it. I didn't even know it was taken from "Change the Beat"; it's just what I used to scratch with.

—Peanut Butter Wolf

While it was Hancock's name on the video credit and record sleeve, D.ST's distinctive scratching stole the show from the seasoned jazz veteran. Yet had it not been for D.ST's previous single, 1982's "Grandmixer Cuts It Up" via the Celluloid label, another DJ might have gotten to chance to shine in that spotlight.

I was commissioned by Herbie Hancock to do a couple of tracks. And I thought it would be more interesting to do something more contemporary, related to what was going on in New York with street music at the time. I went to Bambaataa and asked him who would be good to play in time, as a soloist. The idea was to use the turntable as the solo instrument in the breaks as you would a guitar or saxophone. He suggested Whiz Kid and D.ST. I knew D.ST because we'd already started doing records with him, so there was a relationship. I grabbed him, set up a track in Brooklyn, and he soloed in the breaks.

—Bill Laswell (coproducer of Future Shock)

"Rockit" climbed only as high as number seventy-one on the *Billboard* singles chart. But thanks to an eye-popping stop-action animation video by directors Godley & Creme, the song proved enormously successful on the fledgling MTV network, leaving a lasting impression on a generation of DJs to come.

Before "Rockit," my view toward the art was really limited. All you could do was take two records and blend them together, maybe take words and juggle them back and forth, the way Flash used to back in the day—"Good times . . . good times . . ."—and that was my scope of the turntable, up until then. But the scratches on "Rockit" weren't just put there for the sake of there being scratches; they played a big role in the workings of the song. I started to realize you could do more with a turntable. You just had to apply yourself to the turntable as if

it were a musical instrument. Don't look at it as this mechanism that you play records on. You could express yourself
through it.

—Rob Swift

We did two tracks [with D.ST], "Earth Beat" and "Rockit." At that
time, "Good Times" was the track everybody was using to say
"good"; "fresh" came from Fab 5 Freddy's "Change the Beat." So
on "Rockit," "good" and "fresh" became the back-and-forth cut.
On "Earth Beat," he used some alternative vinyl we'd supplied.
One of them was a gamelan record, and some other avant-garde
noise records, maybe even Stockhausen. Recording was really,
really quick, like instant. The driver who brought him from the
Bronx waited on the couch while we did the whole thing.

—Bill Laswell (coproducer of Future Shock)

Unfortunately, the legacy of D.ST's achievement would be slow
in progressing further. As record companies large and small began to
appreciate rap fans as a source of untapped consumer dollars, hip-
hop became big business. MCs were pushed farther into the limelight, and DJs often had to make do backing up the man or woman
on the microphone from the shadows at the side of the stage.
Although sometimes these collaborations were remarkable (Mark the
45 King's work with Queen Latifah; Terminator X's invaluable contribution to Public Enemy), many observers felt the DJ's craft was at
an impasse. Instead of progressing to making revolutionary solo
albums that built on the innovations of Flash and D.ST, most DJs
had to be content with the odd rapless turn buried on an MC's long-
player.

The record companies started doing what we call the Whispering
Devil in the Zulu Nation, whispering in the rappers' ears. "You
don't need your DJs—y'all are the ones who['re] the stars!" Next

MEET THE DJ

Peanut Butter Wolf

Most fourth graders devote their free time to playing video games, watching TV, or playing sports. But Bay Area beatmeister Chris Manak—alias Peanut Butter Wolf—began preparing for his career early. "I started buying records in 1979," he recalls, "when I was nine years old." Stacks of funk and soul singles littered his room. For his thirteenth birthday, he asked for a mixer so he could interface two ancient turntables he'd acquired. His parents obliged, splurging at the local Radio Shack.

Inspired by Grandmixer D.ST's scratch solos on Herbie Hancock's "Rockit," Manak learned to fashion his own mixes. Slowly, he emerged from the confines of the bedroom to sharpen his skills in public, first as a mobile DJ, then later on radio, and finally as a recording artist, under the name Chris Cut.

In 1988, Chris Cut turned into Peanut Butter Wolf (borrowing the tag from the bogeyman tormenting his girlfriend's little brother) and divided his time between performing in a punk band and laying down hip-hop beats with MC Charizma. The latter project eventually yielded a major label deal, but the artists soon found themselves at cross-purposes with the people signing their checks. Unfortunately, these differences became moot after the tragic shooting of Charizma in 1993.

Peanut Butter Wolf resurfaced with an instrumental album, Peanut Butter Breaks, on his own Stone's Throw label, followed by the EP *Lunar Props*. But it was his contributions to the compilations *Return of the DJ* (the haunting history lesson "The Chronicles") and *Deep Concentration* that raised his profile outside the underground, positioning him alongside other emerging turntablists like the X-ecutioners and Invisbl Skratch Piklz.

As a DJ, Peanut Butter Wolf gained national exposure when he hit the road with Cut Chemist for a tour of riveting tag-team sets in 1998. Lately his energies have been devoted to nurturing Stone's Throw (which recently launched a series of one-off 45s by artists including Biz Markie and Rob Swift) and promoting his second full-length, *My Vinyl Weighs a Ton*.

thing you know, they started leaving the DJs and the turntables and going to DAT.

—Afrika Bambaataa

In the early '90s, most rap groups got away from the DJs. Everybody was coming out and doing stuff on DAT. That was horrible! One thing I'll say for Young Black Teenagers, we always went off of vinyl. That's what it was all about.

—DJ Skribble

For a while the MCs weren't even having scratching in their choruses. Part of it was the industry, and the money. For whatever reason, a lot of MCs didn't think it was worth it to split their money with DJs. People started feeling that the DJs were replaceable.

—Peanut Butter Wolf

I was always really saddened by that. It was great when you got a Big Daddy Kane or Biz Markie album and there was a DJ track on there. It gave an album a different angle. Even to this day, when I listen to a rap record, I listen to the beats and then decide if the rap is all right or not; never the other way around.

—Andy Smith

When I was going to rap shows, the DJ wasn't really doing anything new. I got tired of it. Until you had guys like Cash Money come in and change things around, it was just monotonous. How long could you sit and watch someone DJ? You can't really dance to it. The DJ just went poof and went away.

—Kurtis Mantronik

Of course, there's nothing like a little friendly competition to turn up the fire under someone's lazy butt. Not surprisingly, the key force in promoting and popularizing advances in the DJ's art throughout the lackluster '80s was the tradition of DJ battles. Just like square-offs in Jamaica or the Bronx, or between jazz musicians of an earlier era (coincidentally, in jazz circles such duels are sometimes called *cutting*, a synonym for *scratching*), contests between new contenders and established champions pushed everyone to set their sights higher.

As hip-hop moved out of the Bronx, so did DJ battles. Grand-scale competitions on regional, national, and even international levels, including the (now defunct) New Music Seminar's (NMS) Battle for World Supremacy and the DMC World Championship, provide leaders in the field with a chance to show off fresh tricks and mixes. Every year, new developments return home with victors and losers alike, adding one more dimension to the skills at a DJ's disposal.

> There are scratches I invented that I never got credit for. Breaking up the words into syllables? I invented that! I was in the '86 New Music Seminar battle, and the next thing I know, tons of people [were] doing it.
>
> —Prince Paul

> I entered the old DMC heat when I was seventeen. You'd do a four-minute mix. There was a technique people used to use, putting little sticky labels on the actual vinyl, so you could drop the needle on the label and let it slide in to the groove in exactly the right place. Little things like that helped me get it cued up quick, so you could basically do the whole thing without head-phones. But it took time to get the sticky bits in the right groove.
>
> —Liam Howlett

The DMC (short for Disco Mix Club) is an organization with branches in over thirty countries, which hosts contests at several levels, culminating in the annual world championship. Although originally designed as a showcase for mixing skills only, in 1986 New Jersey's DJ Cheese integrated scratching into his mix and upset the DMC applecart forever. Since then, trailblazers, including Cash Money, Invisbl Skratch Piklz, and the X-men (now the X-Ecutioners), have used exposure received as DMC champs to push both DJ culture and their own reputations forward. More recently, a cadre of established insiders launched the International Turntablist Federation (ITF), which hosts its own events, hoping to steal some thunder from the DMC, which has been criticized for reaping financial rewards off hip-hop while making minimal return investments.

However, although battles are an integral part of the turntablism scene, participation is hardly mandatory. Some of the scene's best-known proponents eschew them entirely.

> I'm not very competitive-natured. I dedicate half of my time to DJing and half to making music. To be a battle DJ, you have to practice a certain number of hours a day. It's like the Olympics: you have to be really dedicated and always doing it.
>
> —Peanut Butter Wolf

Although New York remained the hub of hip-hop culture throughout the '80s, other important communities began to emerge. A little farther down the East Coast, in the City of Brotherly Love, a fresh crop of jocks—Cash Money, Jazzy Jeff, Code Money, and Spinbad—were taking DJing in new directions. Code Money's cuts with gangsta rap pioneer Schooly D. were far harsher than D.ST or Flash's early collages. Inspired by the new Philly styles, in 1989 New Yorker DJ Premier's moody, melancholy "DJ Premier in Deep Concentration" (from Gang Starr's *No More Mr. Nice Guy*) made a marked departure from fast-pasted daredevil cutups, showing a more reflective approach to turntable composition that in turn influenced newcomers like DJ Shadow.

Cash Money and Jazzy Jeff both enjoyed successes working with MCs. In particular, DJ Jazzy Jeff, working with rapper the Fresh Prince (aka actor Will Smith), scored five Top 20 pop hits between 1988 and 1993, including "Parents Just Don't Understand." But more importantly, Cash (the 1988 DMC world champ) and Jeff developed a brand new type of scratching: transforming.

In transforming, the DJ cuts the sound on and off with one hand on the fader while scratching the record with the other one. The rapid motion, like flicking a light switch quickly to create a strobe light effect, chops the record into an even finer dice, creating complex polyrhythms. Transforming caught on with DJs in very short order.

At the time, it was Jazzy Jeff and Cash Money, two guys out of Philly. Cash Money was the guy who came up with the transforming type of scratching, the really fast manipulation. A lot of people copied that from him, but he never really got the recognition that he should have. He came up with those razor-sharp cuts. He was doing different types of scratches, making it more entertaining. And then other people took over, because they would see him in competitions.

—Kurtis Mantronik

I was talking to Cash Money a couple of weeks ago and he told me that what he does when he scratches is he takes on the attitude of a singer. What he's trying to do is riff the way a singer would, but scratching. Sometimes while he's scratching over a beat, he has a song in his head. He may be thinking about an old Gladys Knight song and try to scratch her vocals in a way. That's pretty deep.

—Rob Swift

In the early '90s, the Bay Area of California began to emerge as a hotbed for innovative DJs and the notion of turntablism coalesced more clearly. Distanced from the mainstream hip-hop communities of Los Angeles and the East Coast, and blessed with a tradition of ambitious independent music, the San Francisco region hosted a wealth of mobile party DJs during the mid-'80s, and local battle culture was fertile with talent.

In 1991, a S.F. crew dubbed FM 2.0 burst onto the national competition circuit. Instead of the flashy acrobatics that were the stock in trade of high-profile competition jocks at the time, members Apollo, Q-Bert, and Mixmaster Mike dazzled judges and audiences with orchestrated scratch routines and tricks developed in the relative isolation of the Bay Area. They took the scene by storm, and after snagging the world championship crown three years in a row, they were asked by the DMC to please bow out of future competitions. Over the course of time, and with the addition of new members, FM 2.0 became the West Coast Rocksteady DJ Crew, and eventually Invisbl Skratch Piklz.

Important like-minded individuals and posses emerged concurrently with or shortly after the Piklz: L.A.'s Beat Junkies, London's Scratch Perverts, New York quartet the X-Men. Although San Francisco remains an important epicenter for turntablism (largely owing to releases by independent record labels like Om, Bomb Hip-Hop, and Asphodel), unity between leaders of the scene and their desire to advance the art have slowly but surely made this an international phenomenon and revitalized contemporary hip-hop.

> There was a low period, a time when you couldn't really find DJs who could make a great set. With Rob Swift and Skratch Piklz and Beat Junkies and X-ecutioners, it's started to come back. It's a whole new movement. But they all have one thing in common. They all respect the roots of those ideas, and where it came from. All those kids have a really strong sense of history.
> —Bill Laswell (coproducer of Future Shock)

> As a result of the neglect the industry showed them, and the way the culture was going, a lot of the people we looked up to were disgust[ed]. They were still active, battling and doing stuff musically, but they took a step back politically and were watching what was going on. We said, "We can't let this happen . . . you can't forget about these guys!" If you read magazine articles on us, one

177

thing we always talk about is the people that came before us and laid down the law. We became responsible for exposing people to the fact that if it wasn't for people like Flash, like [DJ] Theodore, D.ST, Cash Money, and Stevie D, the art of DJing wouldn't have grown as much as it did. There wouldn't even be hip-hop. We're just trying carry the torch.

—Rob Swift

Although the arsenal of tricks at the disposal of today's turntablist is formidable, the essentials boil down to two categories: scratching and beat juggling. In and of themselves, these gimmicks can quickly grow tiresome, but when executed with inspiration they allow for much greater variety of sound manipulations.

The number of different scratches introduced since DJ Theodore first discovered the basics boggles the mind. Most of them boast names reminiscent of '60s dance crazes: the Tweak (a staple of Mixmaster Mike's sound), the Scribble (holding the record still while tensing arm muscles, causing the record to vibrate quickly while the needle scratches a very limited surface area), the Banana (flexing the record while moving it), and the Hydroplane (using a free finger to apply counterpressure against the record's rotation).

The Crab and the Flare are two of the most popular scratches. The latter, developed by S.F. DJ Flare, is essentially transforming in reverse, starting with the sound turned *on* at the beginning of the scratch instead of *off*, thus requiring less movement on the fader. In the Crab, a four-click Flare (perfected by Q-Bert and DJ Disk), the DJ hits the fader with each individual finger to turn the sound on while applying reverse pressure with the thumb to cut the sound back off.

Beat juggling was first promoted by Stevie D and debuted at the 1990 NMS Battle for World Supremacy. Isolating favorite sounds on two records, the DJ plays one snippet, then cuts to the other while reversing the first, then cuts back again, creating a loop. Depending on how the record is controlled, tempos can be sped up or slowed down, syncopation created, and short passages elongated beat by beat. In a Breakdown, the DJ manually slows down each record, pausing rotation on each beat count in a rhythm. To create a Strobe, the jock must breakdown two copies of the same record simultaneously; one copy plays a step ahead of the other, and the turntablist must alternate playback between the two channels.

Does all this sound hopelessly confusing? Well, so does jujitsu, gourmet cooking, or even knitting, on the printed page. Like any aspect of the DJ's trade, scratching mastery is attained via a keen eye and hours hunched over your decks. Don't shy away from being resourceful. Scratching is like eating with chopsticks—as long as the desired end result is achieved, then whatever technique employed is "right" for you.

> I'm not really good at doing Crabs. I've got my own way of doing them, which isn't the same way as everybody else's. Nobody can do Crabs like Q-Bert can. But I'm a club DJ, and I don't need all the ridiculous skills to perform in a club . . . just some of them.
> —Andy Smith

Thanks to an explosion of how-to videos and ready-made battle records (often products created by folks like the Piklz themselves), tackling the craft has never been easier. DJs like Kid Koala and A-Trak are already at the peak of their game, even though they're barely out of their teens. Yet some vets fret that youngsters might be better served by longer stints in the trenches and less time spent maintaining the status quo. With so many tricks to master, are musicianship and individuality are being sacrificed on the altars of technical precision and big prizes? Divorced from a musical aesthetic, scratching and beat juggling can quickly tax an audience's attention, no matter how impressive the DJ's execution may be.

> The new kids coming up aren't spending enough time learning the basics. They get involved in DJing, and all of the sudden they want to learn the most technical scratches, because that's what

they see on videos and hear on the mix tapes. They don't appreciate that understanding the basics of it all helps you be a better DJ because you understand why those scratches sound the way they do, as opposed to just doing them.

—Rob Swift

Something might sound like it's difficult to do, but it's not always pleasing to the ear if you've heard it too many times.

—Peanut Butter Wolf

Unfortunately, a lot of the new-school kids who are calling themselves turntablists and not DJs anymore think that to be a good DJ, you have to do Flares and Crabs, and all these technical scratches. When you're a good DJ, you can mix any kind of music and rock any kind of party. I can cut and do tricks, and I'll throw that into the show, but I'm not going to do it for four hours straight. You can't just wow people with tricks for twenty minutes. These turntablist kids have so much talent, but if you threw most them into a club situation for four hours, they'd be lost.

—DJ Skribble

I remember this guy I saw at a club frantically scratching away, and he was brilliant, really tight. But he was talking to his friends while he was doing it. It was so funny to see, I just had to laugh. That's when I realized there's more to it than just having technique.

—Jonathan More (Coldcut)

In one way, I can really respect people like the Skratch Piklz. It's incredible stuff that they can do, and the way they do it is really great. But in another way, there's something conservative to it. We were spinning together at a Beastie Boys show in London. And there were other DJs, like the Scratch Perverts from England. In my opinion, at this show, it was becoming too technical. It reminded me a bit—and maybe I'm not being fair—of guitar solos.

Alec Empire

It should also be noted that the unwieldy term *turntablism* has not been embraced wholeheartedly by all DJs, even in the hip-hop community. Some worry that accepting the tag will place limiting parameters around a style rich with infinite possibilities. But on the other hand, the name distinguishes the craft of making music with turntables, which is technically more demanding, from the more common practice of playing records.

Turntablism is obviously more technical than being able to mix. Considering the amount of time and skill put into it, it's fucked up that it isn't widely recognized and appreciated in the world of your basic club DJs, especially in England. But to someone who's an outsider, listening to it on the records, it sounds like a disjointed record that isn't sequenced properly. They don't understand what's actually happening. Until you see it, it's just impossible to picture, one guy doing the bass line, one guy doing the beats....

—Liam Howlett

Ultimately, if turntablism is to continue maturing with vitality, it must be understood as one point on the line of musical continuity, with considerations of both past history and future potential to take into account and a tradition of innovation to uphold.

I'm blessed to be from the era I came up in—the '80s—when the basics were all we were doing: backspinning, scratching here and there, blending two records together. As it got more complicated and complex, I grew with the art. In terms of years, now the art is basically in its teens, but people aren't learning about what it was like [before] its adolescence.

—Rob Swift

I love DJing and I'll always do it; that's my instrument. But there are so many new guys that are just sick that it's hard to deal with. Look at A-Trak—the kid's sixteen and doing backflips. That's cool. Let those kids take over. I'm going to be making the records they're scratching with.

—DJ Lethal

I learned how to DJ at a time when a fewer people were doing it and it was a lot less intimidating to try. The standards are much higher now. I'm intimidated by a lot of the young guys. I almost feel like I'm set in my ways in terms of scratching and turntable manipulation. I like to learn from the young guys, yet at the same time I have my own style. Everybody has their own thing they can add to the movement.

—Peanut Butter Wolf

10 The Music That We Make

I respect DJs who create great music and who have the courage
to be different.

—Mixmaster Morris

Although turntablism has prompted the public to view DJs in
a different light, the evolution of the DJ as a musician—a conductor,
composer, or performer of music—has continued unabated since the
emergence of disco and hip-hop in the '70s. DJs invented and refined
a staggering variety of musical styles—house, techno, electro, drum
and bass—throughout the '80s and '90s. Americans, still suffering
from their foolish "disco sucks" hangover, banished many of these
developments chiefly to the underground, whereas in Europe, dance
music is pop. Even so, songs spawned from these various genres, from
the infectious house of Crystal Waters ("Gypsy Woman") to the goofy
post-rave techno of the KLF ("Justified and Ancient," with Tammy
Wynette) have penetrated the U.S. pop charts at periodic intervals,
slowly indoctrinating the mainstream.

An in-depth discussion of the history and development of every
significant DJ-driven music genre since the '70s could take up several more volumes of prose. Fortunately, other authors braver than I
have already tackled this task in recent years (most notably, Simon
Reynolds, in his comprehensive *Generation Ecstasy: Into the World of*

Techno and Rave Culture). Rather than repeat that material, I've opted for quick snapshots from the records and trends that set the stage for today's state of affairs. And then we'll get up to our elbows in the applications and implications of the DJ's art for contemporary DJs who record and play original music.

Being a DJ is all about making connections: segues between records, links between genres, and a bond with an audience. This same philosophy, transformed and expanded, has underscored every significant development in dance music. For a shining example, we need look no further than 1982's "Planet Rock" by Afrika Bambaataa and Soul Sonic Force.

"Planet Rock," created with the help of keyboard player John Robie, producer Arthur Baker, and Tommy Boy Records head Tom Silverman, was a natural extension of the global consciousness that already informed both Bambaataa's DJ sets and the Zulu Nation. Aiming to bring the excitement of rap to wider audiences, without compromising its original spirit, Bambaataa lifted the melody from Kraftwerk's "Trans-Europe Express," plus the rhythm track from their later cut, "Numbers," then folded in breaks from staples like "Super Storm" by Captain Sky and "The Mexican" by Babe Ruth. The resulting gold record brought Düsseldorf, Germany, and the South Bronx much closer and left an indelible stamp on dance music on both sides of the Atlantic.

> A lot of people think Kraftwerk was my biggest influence. I give Kraftwerk, Yellow Magic Orchestra, and Gary Numan [respect], but that was just one part of my sound. My main influences [are] James Brown, Sly and the Family Stone, and George Clinton. When I got into electronic music, I looked around and said, "There ain't no black people doin' this!" I wanted to create an electronic sound, with a lot of funk and heavy bass added.
> —Afrika Bambaataa

Similar musical sentiments to Bambaataa's would surface almost concurrently in Detroit. Weaned on a diverse diet of electronic music, from Clinton's Parliament/Funkadelic to Giorgio Moroder and Gary Numan, teenagers Juan Atkins, Derrick May, and Kevin Saunderson forged a new sound dubbed techno (borrowed from a song title, "Techno City," by Atkins early outfit Cybotron). As mobile DJs at parties hosted by affluent black teenagers, Atkins, May, and their colleague Eddie Fowlkes had mastered whipping their discriminating audiences into frenzies by mixing "progressive" European disco tracks from acts like Capricorn and Klein & M.B.O. alongside British synthesizer pop and underground New York disco à la D-Train. When all four men started releasing original tracks, the resulting music distilled these influences (and Detroit's exhausted urban landscape) into a Spartan electronic sound that paired chilly futurism with a compelling beat and had a surprising potential for emotional resonance.

> Detroit has made some of the most interesting and inspired music of the last century.
>
> —Richie Hawtin (Plastikman)

Meanwhile, in Chicago, disco had continued going strong in the underground (again, largely with black, gay audiences) long after the furor of Comiskey Park had subsided. Whereas Detroit's rhythmic underpinnings favored funk, in Chicago the four-on-the-floor beat still reigned. But in the absence of new disco records, Chicago DJs like Frankie Knuckles, Ron Hardy, and Jesse Saunders—as well as radio's legendary Hot Mix Five (Farley "Jackmaster" Funk, Steve "Silk" Hurley, Ralphi Rosario, Mickey Oliver, and Kenny Jason)—made do recycling materials. Throwing Philadelphia International and Salsoul classics into the mix, they edited breaks on reel-to-reel tapes and extended songs with duplicate copies, giving birth to a sound dubbed house (in homage to the Warehouse, where Knuckles held court from 1977 to 1983).

> The thing that made Frankie special was that he got music that nobody else in town had. While we were playing Cory Daye's "Pow Wow" and France Joli's "Come to Me"—which are great songs—he was playing cool New York stuff, like Loose Joints and Taana Gardner.
>
> —Jesse Saunders

Competing for crowds, DJs augmented and modified their approaches, adding sound effects (like Knuckles' patented steam locomotive noises) and drum machines; in time, that kick drum would personify house. Later, elements like piano riffs, mechanized handclaps, and hissing hi-hats would further codify the sound. The earliest house tracks, like Jesse Saunders's "On and On," captured all the elements on vinyl, melding snippets of classic melodies with these simple but effective rhythmic tricks. When more song-oriented cuts like "Love Can't Turn Around" crossed over on to the British pop charts in 1986, house was on its way to redefining European pop music.

> If you look at "On and On," it's basically just a DJ track record. To be honest, I felt really guilty when I made that, because I wasn't writing a song. If people are getting that crazy over some drum tracks and rhythms, what would happen when we did a real song? The rest is history.
>
> —Jesse Saunders

One interesting upshot of these emerging genres taking root in British soil was a slew of records that captured the DJ's role as one who organized the playback of prerecorded sound in a new and exciting fashion. With the advent of cheap sampling technology, throughout 1987 and 1988 hits like "Pump Up the Volume" by M/A/R/R/S, "Beat Dis" by Bomb The Bass, "Theme from S'Express" by S'Express, and "Say Kids (What Time Is It?)" by Coldcut, applied hip-hop's cut-and-paste ethos to a dizzying, often hilarious array of source materials, then grafted the collage atop house-style beats.

> "Wheels of Steel" by Grandmaster Flash and "Lessons 1, 2 & 3" by Double Dee & Steinski inspired us to start making records. A London hip-hop DJ announced a competition, to see who could turn in the best mix, and I spent two weeks making "Say Kids...." Then I thought, *I'm not just going to enter this; it's too good to just give away.* That was when I met Jonathan. He cleverly pointed out that the catchiest bit was where we mixed [James Brown's] "Funky Drummer" with *The Jungle Book,* and suggested that we put an extended version of that on the b side—and he was totally right. When we got it pressed up, he played that side at a club and it was a lot easier to dance to the rather fragmented a side.
>
> —Matt Black (Coldcut)

Although new legal precedents would quickly curtail extensive proliferation of such colorful cuts, the fundamental ideas they popularized—use of old sounds as inspiration for new musical hybrids, the juxtaposition of seemingly incongruous materials to entertain (or arrest)—remain at the heart of much of the contemporary music recorded by DJs.

> There is a constant collage and recycling. Now is the first time everybody realizes we are making repetition and collage. A hundred years ago the Dada movement said that with a mustache on the *Mona Lisa.* And now we admit—as a culture—that we are monkeys and repeat our ancestors.
>
> —DJ Soul Slinger

> We love sample culture. It's where we come from, the postmodern idea of taking this and this and that.
>
> —Tom Rowlands (Chemical Brothers)

I was obsessed with the sampler years before I could possibly afford one. I didn't turn to the turntables as much as the sampler. Back in '85, I said, "We've had a century of making records; that's stage one. Now we sample them."

—Mixmaster Morris

The sampler is only as intelligent as the person using it is. If you want to be creative, then you will; if you don't, then you'll just be lazy.

—Liam Howlett

There are parts in Digital Hardcore recordings that are straight-ahead beats. But also, the sound always is breaking down and collapsing and starting this confusion. They're really cut-ups. That [approach] comes from the DJing style I developed in Berlin with some other people, synchronizing punk records with jungle. At that time, I was also listening to dub and Lee "Scratch" Perry, and that was an important part [of my sound], too. Because sometimes he did edits that were so out of control.

—Alec Empire

Today the concepts of hybrid and collage in DJ music don't just begin and end with dropping a sample of Ofra Haza singing in Hebrew into a hip-hop track (as Coldcut once did on their revolutionary remix of Eric B. & Rakim's "Paid in Full"). For his debut full-length *OK*, UK DJ-producer Talvin Singh solicited performances from singers from Bombay, India and Okinawa, Japan; an orchestra from Madras, India; bassist Bill Laswell; and jazz vocalist Cleveland Watkiss and stitched them all together with drum and bass beats. Japan's DJ Krush works with rappers from Philadelphia and New York, handling U.S. hip-hop and jazz traditions with more respect than many domestic practitioners do. This mentality—the DJ as conductor, the global village as a limitless orchestra—is reflected in approaches to making music and living life that go way beyond swiping James Brown sound bites.

> I didn't like record companies saying, "Oh, you should be just a hip-hop artist." I wanted to do funk with James Brown, and I did it. When I wanted to work with John Lydon or Nona Hendryx, or make reggae with Yellowman, I was just trying to show people that you should never stop artists from working with each other. Although I'm a hip-hop artist, I'm a hip-hop artist and then some.
>
> —Afrika Bambaataa

> I have a studio in Chinatown, and another one up in Chelsea. You turn left, and the signs are in Hebrew from the old Jewish neighborhood. You turn right, they're in Spanish; you go down the street they're in Cantonese; you go up the street, they're in Mandarin. I like the idea of the musicality of the open landscape. That's something I use in a lot of my own work.
>
> —DJ Spooky

Although DJs write and record original music with audiences besides their peers in mind, and sometimes for listeners who may never step foot on a dance floor, many concede that understanding how DJs mix and program and conventional constructions for club tracks influence their own tunes.

> DJing taught me all about structure, when to bring a certain part of a record in, so it's going to make the most impact. And when to take something out of a track, so that when you're mixing the record it doesn't get fucked up.
>
> —Kurtis Mantronik

There are formulas you have to stick to when producing drum and bass. When I'm writing drum and bass, I make a great intro that you can mix into. There will be set arrangements, and a big drop that you really recognize, with a little drum roll going into it; otherwise people don't know when it happens. The sad truth is if you have all that buildup on a drum and bass track, rather than making a tune that falls straight in, you'll sell one thousand extra copies.

—DJ Rap

It drives me nuts that for a seven-minute song, you have to have three minutes of basic mix parts, but that stuff is so necessary. The tracks that get played are the ones that are DJ-friendly. But it's so hard for me to write intros like that! I like to diversify and do odd things. But that would make it impossible to mix, and nobody would play the track.

DJ Tron

My experience as a DJ helps a lot, because the music I make is for DJs. I know that you need the intro, the breakdown. I don't make music for pop radio. I don't produce a track or a remix with the thought that it might have radio crossover potential. I make music for people like me, because I know how happy I am when I go into a record store and find a record that I love.

—Emily Ng

A lot of the time, a DJ will get sent records and only listen to a few seconds of each. You make your judgment that quickly, and if you don't like it, you get rid of it.

—Peanut Butter Wolf

Being a DJ hasn't affected all the aspects of my musical composition, but it definitely has helped. Because when you go to make a club track, you know what kind of records DJs like to hear. Certain things make the difference in whether or not your record is going to get played by certain DJs.

—Juan Atkins

A good DJ is distinguished by his or her ability to hook up with the soul of the crowd. When those skills are translated into making a record, they can be used in a variety of ways: to produce mindless, lowest-com-mon-denominator pap that triggers Pavlovian responses in a audience; to go a step further and toy with ingrained expectations; or look at what hasn't been done and create something different, geared for maximum visceral impact. The best DJ-producers remember that as in program-ming or mixing, peaks and valleys, variety, and a knack for the unex-pected can be crucial when composing original music.

When I'm in the studio, making a six-minute piece of music, it's the same spirit as when I DJ. There are highs and lows, maybe even key changes, within the record.

—Paul Oakenfold

If you put on a record that's one style, one vibe all the way through, it's more easy to listen to. I find that our albums are not listening albums, because there's too much diversity and change. But if we can't maintain some diversity, then dance music is just going to die out.

—Matt Black (Coldcut)

Some of the music that I make is for nightclubs, but not all of it. But I also like to record tracks that you can listen to in your car or while you're vacuuming at home. I was signed to a major label when I was younger, and I started making music for my A&R [Artists & Repertoire] guy, trying to guess what the masses were going to want. It's really important to make music for yourself.

—Peanut Butter Wolf

If you're going to make music you need to find a context in which it might be enjoyed.

—Mixmaster Morris

The future really is the essence and inspiration of this music, so it's always changing. A lot of other types of music don't have that. The mentality of this music is to always push forward, to evolve and change and mutate. Hopefully, that will continue. Every time I start to get bored—and I do have times where I start to have that feeling—another record comes along and "Here we go again!"

—Richie Hawtin (Plastikman)

One advantage a DJ has over a conventional musician is a fairly constant supply of guinea pigs for new material. If a band tries to slip new material into a set, often they're lucky if they can garner even modest applause; audiences haven't had time to become familiar with the tune yet. But since dance music's shelf life is often much shorter, slipping in a new track isn't such a risky proposition for a DJ trying to figure out if they've got their next hit almost finished, or there are bugs yet to be hammered out.

Any artist who can DJ, or vice versa, is at an advantage because he can road test his own tracks. And also get the bird's-eye view of what gets the best response.

—Mixmaster Morris

Sometimes I go have an acetate pressed of a new track. I want to hear it loud. And when you mix [a track] in with other things, it sounds completely different. Also, I like to get a preview of what the crowd thinks. Then I get an idea if I'm going in the right direction.

—DJ Tron

We were DJing every Saturday night while we were making Dig Your Own Hole and making tracks specifically to play on DAT. Just hearing the mix and the sounds in club, the record starts taking on its own life. You can't hear if everything's working when you're stuck in the studio. You only get a clinical version of things. Seeing people reacting to the sounds in the right way is very useful.

—Ed Simons (Chemical Brothers)

But these days, DJs are involved with a lot of musical permutations and combinations that extend beyond the conventional realms of hip-hop and dance music. An increasing number of rock artists are incorporating DJs into their music. From the groovy postmodern pastiche of Beck and Sugar Ray's featherweight pop to the atmospheric trip-hop of Portishead, Limp Bizkit's searing hard rock—hip-hop melange, and the turntablist-Latin fusion of Ozomatli, every style of music imaginable seems to be able to incorporate the DJ's contributions. Even the U.S. stronghold of D.I.Y. indie rock, Olympia, Washington, has embraced the craze, with folks like DJ Wally and DJ Spooky remixing tracks for the Kill Rock Stars label and bands like IQU making turntables an integral part of the lineup.

In some outfits, such as electronic trio Underworld, the DJ's contributions are essential to the band's distinctive sound (before Darren Emerson came on board, Underworld sounded like INXS on bad street drugs). Others seem to feel a DJ's role is just to fill in holes or add to the overall sonic barrage, serving as little more than window dressing. But adding an inventive DJ to an ensemble opens the gate to new areas of musical exploration.

Everybody else in a rock band scratches normal hip-hop sounds that they buy on breakbeat albums. As soon as a DJ gets into a band, his first sound is "fresh … fresh … chnk-chnk-chnk …

MEET THE DJ

DJ Lethal of Limp Bizkit

Being the DJ in a chart-topping band may not be as unusual as it was fifteen years ago, but how many DJs can boast an integral role in the careers of three hit acts? Only one: DJ Lethal. Not bad for a dude who rarely rises before midafternoon.

Born in the republic of Latvia, Leor DiMant immigrated to New York as a child. He began DJing in high school during the mid-'80s. "My dad's record collection inspired me to start. He had everything from Russian waltzes to Tom Brown. I jacked his turntables." He taught himself how to scratch and began distributing mix tapes among friends.

In 1990, Lethal hooked up with rappers Everlast and Danny Boy to form House of Pain (HOP). Their 1992 single "Jump Around" climbed to number three on the charts, but HOP's star began waning after the group's eponymous debut. The trio's 1996 swan song *Truth Crushed to the Earth Shall Rise Again* features some of Lethal's best production work, which sadly went unnoticed owing to poor sales.

After relocating to Los Angeles, Lethal hooked up with then-unknown outfit Sugar Ray, producing their *Lemonade and Brownies* album. Among his other credits, DJ Lethal can be found on releases by Biohazard, Sepultura, and Funkdoobiest, as well as Korn's contribution to the *Spawn* soundtrack.

Lethal's career took a new twist when a production gig with the Jacksonville, Florida, outfit Limp Bizkit (who'd toured with HOP) turned into a full-fledged band membership. Thanks to explosive live shows and a hit video, "Faith," the quintet's debut *Three Dollar Bill, Y'all$*—featuring Lethal's "is-it-a-guitar-or-is-it-a-turntable?" scratching—has become requisite listening for disgruntled teens. The group released their follow-up *Significant Other* this summer. Lethal is also signed individually to Loud Records and is working on an ambitious solo project that, when last we asked, he was contemplating releasing as a quadruple CD!

fresh..." Eeeew! Okay, I scratched a straight word from a Rakim cut on a new Limp Bizkit song, but I haven't done that for two albums...and then it goes into this new scratch I invented that's pretty sick.

—DJ Lethal

If you have a whole band, you don't need two turntables. I try to be another guitar player. But I don't stop and do solos. To me, doing a [turntable] solo on stage is like the guitar player stopping and soloing for twenty minutes. I'm more into the Tom Morello [of Rage Against the Machine] angle, making fucked-up sounds. That's why I go through a Marshall stack, with a bunch of pedals. Before I started, I had never seen a DJ doing that, pumping mad Jimi Hendrix crazy shit.

—DJ Lethal

One lone DJ can even be the impetus for starting a new band!

The Dub Pistols formed totally by accident. I found myself suddenly booked to play main floors [as a DJ] and, to be honest, I wasn't that good. So I started bringing in Lee and Malcolm, scratching on a third deck, so I always had somebody to smooth out the bumps. I was a DJ who needed covering up, and that was the punk ethic in action.

—Barry Ashworth

Like any seasoned performer, a resourceful DJ can move between musical worlds. American rave patrons know Carlos Soul Slinger for his drum and bass sets, but European jazz festival fans are more likely to recognize him because he also spins live in an improvisational jazz ensembles, alongside Anthony Braxton, Derek Bailey, or Elliot Sharp. Likewise, DJ Disk first made his name as a member of the Invisbl Skratch Piklz, but today his turntable résumé makes for a pretty disorienting read: He's worked with Japanese cult favorites MCM & the Monster, sonic experi- mentalists Praxis (featuring Bill Laswell), El Stew, and even the goofy alternative outfit Primus.

> DJ Disk is one of my good friends. We're actually planning to do a crazy new school thing together. I want to make a band with just DJs: one drummer, a bass player, and a guitar player. The Piklz do some stuff like that, but I want to form an actual band, with real songs. I'm talking about making our own records with our own guitar sounds, all in key, not just using stuff that's already out there.
>
> —DJ Lethal

> Lately I've been playing with DJ Disk, who listens closely and is a very innovative musician. He can definitely influence the way you phrase things. Live, a turntablist can be a huge influence on the way you approach notes, phrasing, or an instrument. And because you can't get trapped into playing like someone else with a turntable, it can get you out of clichés. You can play their records, but you can't imitate their character or technique.
>
> —Bill Laswell

DJing can also serve as the foundation for completely original performance practices, an area artists like Coldcut and Detroit techno maestros Richie Hawtin and Jeff Mills have been exploring in greater detail. Building on the early Chicago house traditions of augmenting a track with drum machines or special effects, plus the Detroit school of radically altering a record's sound by adjusting EQ levels, Hawtin's "Decks, EFX & 909" shows are a fusion of DJ set and improvised elec- tronic jam. Meanwhile, Coldcut mixes audio and visual materials live in concert, condensing the symbiosis fashioned between DJ, visuals technician, and crowd at a rave down to the level of the laptop com- puter.

My set's not about playback, really; it's about creation. When Jeff and I start with a 909, we clear what was set earlier and start with nothing. We have our records, but when we start to build, the set changes every night. You never program it exactly the same. We'd like to get to the point where we start with just two machines with nothing in them, and see where we go. Is that different from just playing our own records? It's definitely more interesting.

—Richie Hawtin (Plastikman)

I wanted to show that dance artists could produce a different type of live show [that] wasn't modeled on the rock show. You can take your whole studio out on the road, which is what Orbital does, but that can be pretty boring. And I don't think taking your records out and saying "I'm just going to play my record and mix it, and that's my promotional tool" really says anything, either. What we wanted to do was come up with a combination of all those elements—plus visuals—that was compact enough to be done by just Jon and me. Now we've managed to do that, and it's just a question of making it better. We never rehearsed. We just came up with the concept, got all the hardware working—which was a nightmare—and went straight out on the road.

—Matt Black (Coldcut)

This trend is on the rise. London's Pure Science, alias Phil Sebastian, was appointed best new DJ by *Muzik* magazine in the autumn of 1998, even though turntables have nothing to do with his sets. Nor do CDs or DATs. Pure Science works solely with a drum machine, a keyboard, and an arsenal of hard disks of his original tracks to be played back via computer. Rather than comb record bins for the perfect track, he simply manufactures his own, never playing the same set twice and writing new pieces before every gig.

For many DJ who are also artists or producers, their skills on the decks have translated into distinctive approaches to how they hear or create their own work.

> I listen to every track in a record now, to the smallest, minute details, the littlest cymbal in the background. I separate all the tracks and then put them back together again.
>
> —Jumping Jack Frost

> The knowledge of breaks, of beats and the records, just from being involved in the hip-hop DJ scene, was a big influence on my music. But not necessarily the actual hands-on skills of DJing, but that knowledge of where the roots are, in the old beats—that's the thing that's helped me the most.
>
> —Liam Howlett

> One minute you're playing the beats, going, "Yeah, that's cool." Then you're copying the beats, then you're making your own records. Without actually knowing what it was, I learned about my approach to music from DJing, then applied it to my production. Later on I could apply concepts and definitions to what I'd done, but back then my approach was just "that works."
>
> —Prince Paul

> I am a musician, and I am a producer. It's all the same. As a producer, I'm expressing myself musically on the turntables, the same way I would [DJing] on a Technics 1200. I try to approach the turntable the same way I do the sampler: musically, soulfully. I use different equipment to create a vibe.
>
> —Rob Swift

Occasionally, DJs may find that the same unseen hand that can manifest itself during a particularly inspired set is also influencing the creation of their original music.

A lot of times I'll feel that it's not only me making music. I don't feel like I'm completely in control. I'll come up with a bass line, and then I'll find a horn section that's in the same key, and I almost feel like God's helping me make the beat. The music comes through you more than you go into the music. You can't just do something on command; you have to be inspired.

—Peanut Butter Wolf

With so many DJs cluttering up MTV, magazines, and the pop charts, it's no wonder tons of people view spinning as a shortcut to launching a musical career.

All of the sudden, people don't have to spend a couple years learning how to play a guitar. You can pick up some decks and get on it straight away. For people that are into dance music, that eventually leads to buying a sampler. It seems to be a lot easier [to make tracks] these days. For the people who are out there rockin' the scene—the Chemical Brothers, Underworld, us— it makes our job much more difficult. But that's the way new ideas happen. Some young kid in a bedroom will come out with a great record and then take everything forward.

—Liam Howlett

The proliferation of DJ culture has certainly made it easier for folks to uncover alternate approaches for making their own music, infinitely more entertaining than years of dreary piano lessons or learning to bang out three-chord punk jams on a guitar. But a few first-rate jocks note that you shouldn't devalue the importance of other types of musical training—however conventional they may be. They can pay off in the studio.

> I encourage people to take a music theory class. If you're going to be a DJ, you have to understand you're dealing with music.
>
> —Jesse Saunders

> I was very musical, playing piano, sax, and guitar and even singing in the choir! At sixteen I ran away from school to see the Clash play in London. Punk had a fundamental influence in unexpected ways. It killed off the idea of musical dexterity as a prerequisite for success, which wasn't such a bad thing.
>
> —Mixmaster Morris

> I took a year and a half of jazz improvisation, and that helped me get me rid of some of any rigid, classical thinking in regards to house. [My formal training] comes in handy now that I'm producing. Song structure and phrasing is second nature, where I see people who've been doing this for years, who are well-established producers in the house industry, kind of struggle through a song.
>
> —Emily Ng

> When you start making beats, it's not cool if your shit's out of tune. Most of the time, my shit is out of key anyway, because I'll sample something and slow down the turntable, so automatically it goes to a different pitch. But then everything new is going to be based around that pitch. All the parts are out of key [with the original source], but it's in tune with each other. I'm a scientist, dude: Dr. DJ Lethal.
>
> —DJ Lethal

11 Stars

There are so many different reasons to become a DJ now. I can't say they're right or wrong. But most of the DJs in the beginning got into it because of a love of music. There was no other reason. It wasn't to make money or become famous or fly around the world. That wasn't an option. But now it is. There [are] a lot more ulterior motives for these kids.

—Richie Hawtin (Plastikman)

The majority of young DJs are all about the fame, the money, and the three hours of playing all the latest, obvious records.

—Paul Oakenfold

Want proof that DJs today are celebrities? Look no further than Madison Avenue. From Giorgio Armani fashions to Absolut vodka, high-profile vendors in pursuit of a cutting-edge image have started incorporating DJs into how they do business, sponsoring DJ tours and hiring them to spin at stores and parties.

Not long ago, even the most popular DJs walked unrecognized through the city streets, and often even their own places of employment. In a poll conducted by England's *The Face* magazine, only three percent of ordinary citizens surveyed could identify the Chemical Brothers, despite their chart successes. But today, DJs' mugs are plastered on posters and in magazine ads, as spokesmodels for everything from CD mixers (Junior Vasquez) and headphones (Goldie) to eyeglasses (DJ Spooky) and Caterpillar boots (DJ Rap).

That's not to say that DJs displaying the requisite charisma, talent, or petulant behavior to be considered celebrities didn't exist ten, fifteen, even twenty years ago. But back then, their circle of influence was much smaller. Francis Grasso, Larry Levan, and Grandmaster Flash were indisputably stars, but only to fans of the music they helped popularize; in Europe, the trend was virtually nonexistent.

> Apart from a very, very few elite soul DJs, who had a slight following with a predominantly black crowd, there weren't any name DJs at all [in the '70s and early '80s] in Bristol. You went to a club because it was a club. You didn't know the name of the DJ at all.
>
> —Andy Smith

> As far as the public went, they weren't there to give you adulation; you were there to celebrate them. You really had to please them. I've always firmly believed that we were just instruments. The crowd really moved you, and you picked whatever record you did. Those decisions aren't conscious. And any DJ who doesn't think that isn't a DJ—he's an ego-tripper. And probably not much fun to be around, in or out of a club.
>
> —Steve D'Acquisto

Although the emergence of the DJ-as-celebrity on both sides of the Atlantic has been gradual, one obvious growth spurt coincided with the UK rave explosion of 1988. During the Summer of Love, DJs like Carl Cox and Danny Rampling spun for enormous English crowds just discovering dance music for the first time. With the drug Ecstasy added to the equation, a good set became a transcendental experience for many attendees. In pursuit of duplicating it, they often trekked long distances to hear key DJs again and again.

People go to their first club, they take their first E, and that is their music. They're locked into it. It will take another big experience to move them, for it all to make sense...or for their hero DJ to drop.

—Barry Ashworth

All of the sudden the DJs were the megastars, weren't they? They were getting crowds as big as rock bands, in one summer. Ultimately, that must have helped everybody. I can remember years and years when I wasn't getting paid anything. It's a nice feeling to get paid now.

—Andy Smith

People used to come to the club, regardless of the DJ. Our door would never fluctuate that much. A lot of [the celebrity phenomenon] came from up north, because they started paying big money for DJs, and fees started to go up. They were treated like stars, and they started to believe it. At the time a name—Andy Weatherall was big—meant you'd make an extra two hundred or three hundred [pounds] easy, so [the fee] was justified. But there were so many other DJs, and people were going out constantly.

—Barry Ashworth

By the 1990s, DJs had replaced supermodels as the new "hot" celebrities. Today you can't swing a record bag without hitting someone claiming to be a DJ. You'll find them on MTV, in videos and original programs; in television commercials for tennis shoes, soda pop, and big chains like McDonalds; in movies like *Go!* and *Party Girl*; on the sales floors of boutiques; and at fashion shows, private parties, and Hollywood movie premieres. Even the World Championship Wrestling *Monday Nitro* program features the cutting and scratching of DJ Ran!

No wonder kids from Maine to Albuquerque are bypassing adolescent guitar fantasies to head straight for the decks. Once upon a time, being a successful DJ might lead to work as a remixer, producer, or recording artist. Now there are DJs who model and host television programs. Two of the leading house DJs—Junior Vasquez and Frankie Knuckles—are actually penning memoirs! Can the *Martha Stewart Living* pictorial profile of DJ Spooky's all-silver downtown loft be far behind?

In the UK, a DJ is today's pop star. You've got more people going to clubs to watch DJs week in and week out than you have going to watch bands. You've got a million people going to clubs every weekend. That's why bands like U2 and Rolling Stones approach me. I toured with U2 for a year as their opening act. Those are open-minded people who are aware of change, which is generally a curse in life—in anything. The negative people, the people who are afraid—and there are quite a lot in music—don't want to accept that change. That's where the problem occurs.

—Paul Oakenfold

The difference between DJing and a rock concert is that at a rock concert, the audience is passive: *Thank you; the song's over; you can applaud now.* In the club/party atmosphere, it's a lot more democratic. People are really what make the party. Everyone who attends contributes their energy and their dancing to the motion and to the dynamic. The DJ is supplying the music that will help that chain reaction be possible. But I don't think that [DJs] should consider themselves the centerpiece.

—François K.

The transformation of the DJ, from this lonely creature between the bathroom and the cloakroom into a replacement of the rock star, was a natural marketing evolution. But I still feel that the underground DJ is the DJ closer to the region. They're the most important. I'm close to New York. *The* DJ in Seattle is close to Seattle. They are the real DJs.

—DJ Soul Slinger

People in the media describe DJs becoming pop stars as changing something, changing the rock structure. But that's wrong. They just got absorbed [into the system]. You have people playing other people's music, and they get idolized even worse.

—Alec Empire

Amidst all this ballyhoo, there are plenty of seasoned DJs and club patrons these days who temper their excitement for the DJ's rise by echoing Public Enemy's classic battle cry: "Don't Believe the Hype!"

The one thing that gets my back up is [in England] a lot of DJs get rated as being so good. They're taking drugs like there's no tomorrow, and they think they're good, and the magazines think they should be good, and even the people in the clubs think they're good, because they're off their heads as well. But at the end of the day, they're not actually good.

—Andy Smith

DJs have become the new superstars. Some people live up to the billing, but often it's just the emperor's new clothes. People see the name, so they think the tunes [the DJ's] playing are amazing, when a lot of the time, they're probably not.

—Ben Dubuisson (Purple Penquin)

Just remember: You're a DJ—but that doesn't necessarily make you an artist. Obviously, there are really good DJs who write music, like Darren Emerson [from Underworld]. But then you have these people in Germany that get put on pedestals, with all these lights around them...but they're just playing other people's plastic!

—Liam Howlett

A lot of people at large right now consider themselves incredible DJs, yet they're only able to play one kind of music specifically. They don't know how to drop a jazz record out of the blue, because they're letting themselves be governed by that very formatted way. Because they travel a lot and they don't know what a new audience is going to expect, they feel that they have to play a very homogenous mix. Quite honestly, a lot of DJs don't question themselves. It's just a job, a way to make money quickly. It's better than working at the post office.

—François K.

Actually, considering the fantastic benefits extended to postal employees (to say nothing of the sassy little uniforms with the blue shorts), a lot of wannabe DJs might be much happier seeking employment as mail carriers. Especially if they think spinning records is a high-paying field.

In a 1998 profile on the escalating popularity of DJs, the *New York Times* quoted Tommy Hilfiger's "official" DJ Mark Ronson as earning $500 to $750 for his weekly Friday-night VIP-room gig at a Manhattan club, and $1,500 to $2,000 for high-profile fashion events. They also noted that celebrity DJs like Boy George can charge up to ten times that amount for private engagements.

The reality of the situation is that beginning DJs are lucky if a club is willing to fork over cab fare and a couple of drink tickets for a night's work. And competition is fierce—why should a venue pay a DJ any more than the bare minimum it can get away with when every day there are countless new aspirants willing to work for almost nothing for a shot at the shiny brass ring? Still think you really want to be a DJ? Then start stockpiling the ramen noodles and peanut butter now.

With DJing, you get used to not having [money], living from week to week.

—DJ Rap

At Mudd Club, I was making forty dollars a night for eight hours' work—thirty-four dollars take home, because [the owner] was taking out taxes.

—Anita Sarko

If we were lucky, we made thirty-five, forty dollars a night.

—Steve D'Acquisto

When we started [doing parties] back in '87, we used to get the likes of Andy Weatherall for fifty or a hundred pounds. All DJs were that cheap. Nobody was a full-time DJ. It was a cottage industry. People just did it because that's what they wanted to do.

—Barry Ashworth

There's only a couple of people [in drum and bass], like Goldie, who've really been elevated to that [celebrity] level. When you become involved in the scene, you really have to love it, because it's so much hard work. You're not going to make a lot of money when you're starting out, and you have to make a lot of sacrifices.

—Kemistry (Kemistry & Storm)

You've got to come up through the ranks. You have to be prepared to work for quite a few years before you even start getting established. You do gigs for nothing and spend all your money on records.

—Storm (Kemistry & Storm)

Recent years have also seen the emergence of another trend: the celebrity DJ. With artists as attention-getting as singer Boy George, actress Traci Lords, and ex-Jane's Addiction/Porno for Pyros front man Perry Farrell landing work as DJs, it's no wonder an increasing number of DJs devote more time to selecting what outfit to wear than which tunes to pack. For every ludicrous cartoon character like superstar DJ Keoki who's actually amassed a sufficient following to drown out dreary naysayers, there are half a dozen misguided kids who don't realize that donning holographic pants doesn't actually enhance a DJ's ability to relate to the crowd. If you're gonna play up your image, make sure you've got the goods to back it up.

> When I would DJ, I was always dressed from head to toe. I would wear antique clothing—full Victorian drag or a showgirl costume—and tons of makeup, because that's what we did down South. That's why the B-52s looked the way they did!
>
> —Anita Sarko

But keep in mind that a flashy image can also work against you. Fair or not, polished drag queen DJs like Miss Honey Dijon often have to work harder than their less glamorous peers to earn audiences' respect; crowds are astonished that cross-dressing doesn't encumber a DJ's skills on the decks (although those Lee Press-On Nails can be tricky). If you draw attention to anything other than your abilities as a DJ, prepare to be pigeonholed by the uninformed.

> We have a different image that nobody's ever brought [to the public before], but we didn't want to go through it that way. With us, it was never about "We're one black girl and one white girl!" and "We could really exploit this!" We wanted to play music, be respected for our DJ ability, and ability to entertain a crowd.
>
> —Storm (Kemistry & Storm)

> Whether you're white, black, Asian, or Hispanic, you're a DJ and you're playing good music. And people who like the music should come and see you because they like good music, not because an Asian person should go see an Asian DJ and a black person should see a black DJ.
>
> —Heather Heart

Confidence is key to doing the best job you can, but don't let arrogance overshadow your commitment to music and an audience. Otherwise, you're likely to be pegged as a prima donna. And although there's a certain grandeur to being painted a diva, crowds are a lot less forgiving when you can't put your money where your self-congratulatory mouth is.

We all like being loved. But wanking off and thinking you're the king of the world . . . sets a really bad example.

—Jonathan More (Coldcut)

The arrogance [of certain DJs] annoys me. I won't go into names, because that would be negative. But I've played at a certain club in New York where I've gone into the booth and they've taken the cartridge out of the third turntable, they've turned the sound system down. They're paranoid that I'm going to be better than [the resident DJ]. I went back twice to play there over the years, and they've had that stupid attitude. And that turned me off, and I've refused to play this club again.

—Paul Oakenfold

Professionalism, in my opinion, has always been lacking in a large section of the business. But don't get me on that tangent. If you publish that, I'll never work again. Or I'll have a hit put out on me.

—Robbie Leslie

When I knew I was getting the [Michael Todd Room] at Palladium, I kept my mouth shut. And all these other DJs—DJs that I had helped get the jobs they were at—were giving me attitude, because they were going to work at the Palladium. They were treating me like a has-been—"It's over for you." But all along I knew that I had the job . . . and they didn't.

—Anita Sarko

Since the general public looks to creative artists and celebrities to inspire them, help them decipher their emotions, and escape their daily concerns, it follows that DJs are expected to act larger than life. But how much bravado is reasonable for a DJ to do his or her job at top performance, and how much constitutes being a showoff or a pampered brat? As always, the deciding factor is whether a DJ still plays the most inspiring music possible for audiences. If a DJ does that, then even some pretty extravagant behavior is excusable.

> If you're truly a creative person, you have to stand there and look at what is considered great at that time, and say, "Fuck you—I can do better." Had I been realistic, I could not have come to New York without a job and been so arrogant that I decided I could do better than anybody else.
>
> —Anita Sarko

> You may have more talent than someone who's more successful than you are, so keep working at it. But instead of putting that person—who's trying to take things to the next level—down, realize that they're going to open a door for you. Nobody is going to be able to do this for forever. Funkmaster Flex has made a long career of it. Junior Vasquez is older than dirt, and he still gets five thousand people in his club every week. But only a select few can do that.
>
> —DJ Skribble

> Some DJs right now think of themselves as really big business, because they make all these records, mix all these compilations. But in the process of hyping their names, they forget the roots of what they're supposed to be doing, which is catering to a home crowd. A DJ should always have some kind of a home ground, where they can develop what they want to culturally. A place to

hone their skills to a level where they are really saying something with the music, not just putting together a collection of popular songs, or test pressings, acetates, and unreleased stuff.

—François K.

There is still a whole tribe of DJs that are in it just for the music. You encounter the majority of those people at raves. There's a whole generation of younger DJs, some of whom are horrific, but others are really devoted and great. They're not in it for money or glamour, or to have a publicist advance their career so that they become celebrities.

—Robbie Leslie

I know a lot of people who aren't DJs but buy records, and are fans of the music, and do their own parties in their living rooms with their friends on Saturday night. That's the exact same thing we were doing back then. But for a lot of big DJs, as the scene gets bigger it's becoming more and more of a job. You could always see that in a person. The DJs who are really into the music and up for it are the ones you'll see on the dance floor as well.

—Heather Heart

Don't get an ego. Listen to the music. It plays us more than we play it.

—David Mancuso

Of course, there are plenty of DJs—often in the uppermost eche-lons of success—who eschew grandstanding altogether. Undoubtedly Alex Gifford's DJ slot at the 1998 MTV Music Video Awards broad-cast didn't hurt the record sales of his band Propellerheads, but he still showed up for work in a sweater purchased at a thrift store.

The opportunities for travel and meeting new people a successful DJ career can bring are tremendous rewards in themself.

I'm not the type of DJ or recording artist who tries to play the star role: "I want my limousine . . . bring everything to me." If I'm in Japan, I get out there and go among the people. I want to see your temples, your mosques, your churches, and your community centers. What are the problems in this city? I use all that knowledge to my advantage.

—Afrika Bambaataa

I've gotten to do things so far that I'd never dreamed of. I've been from Israel to Brazil, and all over the country and Europe. I've done more in the short span of my DJ career than most people get to do in their whole lives. I get up every day and do something I love. That's a tremendous gift, and I know it could be taken away like that.

—DJ Skribble

We don't have any great philosophical thoughts about celebrity, except I do find it quite strange, the idea of wanting to hang out in those places famous people go for a drink. We're quite happy at our local pub with our friends.

—Ed Simons (Chemical Brothers)

As informal ministers of music and information, DJs exert more influence than ever at the turn of the century. But DJs who truly aspire to make their mark on history might be happier concentrating on the music and leaving the ugly business of handing out accolades to the professionals. (Everyone knows we're all just frustrated musicians anyway.) Some of the most seminal DJs to date have never been household names, but they shaped the tastes of people who are.

I was a person who visited everyplace. I used to be down at Paradise Garage with Larry Levan, checking out that scene, and at other places that were happening. I was there when Madonna started blowing up. A lot of people came passing through our place before they became stars, and I'm glad to see many of them still pushing and kickin' it today.

—Afrika Bambaataa

There was this group of fourteen-year-old boys and girls that would come in [to Rock Lounge in the early '80s], and they all wanted me to play the stuff that I had been playing at Mudd. But at that time I'd gone out and discovered Fela and African music . . . and the beginnings of rap, and Latin music. But these kids would climb up [in the booth] and ask, "Would you play some of the old punk?" "Yeah, but only if you agree to dance to this other music that I've been finding." So I'd put that on, and they'd form conga lines to make fun of it. Fast forward: I'm interviewing Luscious Jackson and I ask "Who are your influences?" And they said, "You are. You opened up our minds." This British book just came out on the Beastie Boys where they cited me as one of their influences. This group of kids grew up into the Beastie Boys and Luscious Jackson! But you don't realize that's happening at the time. . . .

—Anita Sarko

12 The Future of the Future

It's no wonder some DJs are always late for gigs; in the DJ's universe, linear time is a pretty elastic concept. Songs are extended in trance-inducing jams or truncated to an isolated vocal outburst or breakbeat; harmonic progressions meant to imply a sense of forward motion in Western music can be suspended for minutes at a time or abandoned entirely.

Concerns of history are different, too. The milieu of the DJ is an oral tradition, handed down through records and the fashion in which the individual chooses to present them. If a DJ can make music from the '70s, the '60s, or even earlier eras seem vibrant in playback today, who can say those records are dead? Likewise, DJs are often the creators and conduits for sounds so unexpected and new they haven't even been named yet.

With all this in mind, we asked our panel of experts for their thoughts on what developments the immediate future holds for DJs. The answers spanned a gamut of concerns, from mediums of playback and shifts in cultural attitudes to equipment that blurs distinctions between being "just a DJ" and being an original musician, toying with ideas of authorship even further.

When CDs began replacing vinyl LPs as the format of choice in the late '80s, many DJs panicked. Yet ten years later, vinyl remained the undisputed primary medium for DJs of all stripes. For some, the attachment is a sonic concern, for others, it's more sentimental. Considering that most of us own record collections well into the thousands, is it any wonder we're reluctant to switch over? And besides, who'd buy all that secondhand wax?

> I really prefer the sound of vinyl. I will DJ with CDs, but the lion's share of my stuff, and that includes current music, is still in vinyl format.
>
> —Robbie Leslie

> I don't like CDs. They did an experiment that's very scary. They made a recording of birds singing in analog. When they played it back in analog, the real birds would sing along. When they made the recording into a CD, the birds didn't sing back to the music.
>
> —David Mancuso

> As long as the drum and bass scene is still alive, vinyl can't die.
>
> —Kemistry (Kemistry & Storm)

> We've kept one whole plant open and alive in this country, at EMI. The whole drum and bass scene is all cut at the same plant now. It was going to close before the drum and bass scene. And they're very happy to keep pressing our vinyl. I can't see hip-hop people wanting vinyl to die, and if we've got them boys behind us as well, we're cool. We'll just link arms together across the water, and get all the famous people into it, because vinyl is not dying, no way!
>
> —Storm (Kemistry & Storm)

> A house DJ [who] plays house [who] still trumpets vinyl as the ultimate for playing house really ought to wake up. Things are moving on. There are lots of variables to manipulate now. But I

still like playing seven-inch singles now and then; I might even get a few 78s out one day.

           —Jonathan More (Coldcut)

One of the biggest advantages that vinyl affords DJs is a hands-on, physical experience. DJs learn early on not to be afraid to touch their records, to use a gentle push or momentary tug to align rhythms in the mix. And the same criticism leveled at the difference between album cover art in the vinyl era versus today holds true for the technical side of DJing—it's less compelling to look at when the scale is reduced. Watching a DJ pull twelve-inches out of a crate and slap them on the decks might grow dull after a spell, but it sure trumps looking at some bozo slide CDs into a player and twiddle a few knobs.

I always use vinyl. I wouldn't mind DJing with CDs, but it would take getting used to. The hardest thing is that you can't touch the CD. You've got to use that pitch [control], and if you get severely out [of synch], you've almost got to start your mix over from the top. You've got to know how to cue it and drop it on the one.

           —Juan Atkins

Having a piece of vinyl in your hand, being able to touch it and see it, feels so right. It's a part of you, an extension of what you're doing. That's why vinyl's got to stay. If CDs take over, we'll lose that art. Battling with your tunes to get the ultimate mix down is a physical thing, and the crowd enjoys it. Maybe the track comes in slightly off and then you get it on, and they hear that and really get into the mix. It'll be a shame if CDs take over. That's something we dread...

           Storm (Kemistry & Storm)

. . . Even though we've made one.

           —Kemistry (Kemistry & Storm)

Mix CDs are okay—you can't put that on vinyl.

—Storm (Kemistry & Storm)

The turntable is such a key part of my whole musical realm. My turntable is always on my right. It's attached to me. Whether it's for sampling or scratching or just listening, it's there. My CD and DAT and cassette players are far, far away . . . but my turntable is right here.

—DJ Lethal

Someone said to me, "Vinyl is great, but the music is even better." I do love vinyl. For years I was saying, "Vinyl's not going to last another ten years; we['d] better get prepared to move out," but now I'm not so sure. I've changed my mind slightly. This MP3 business is coming to a resolution, and it's evident that CDs don't really have much future. There's nothing attractive about them; they're just some bytes on a bit of plastic.

—Matt Black (Coldcut)

And yet perhaps these are the cries of dinosaurs before the big chill. There are plenty of DJs who eschew vinyl entirely, opting to go the CD route, who move their audiences with just as much aplomb as any vinyl junkie. For many young people growing up today, that slab of black plastic is as antiquated as an 8-track tape. I have a favorite T-shirt printed with the image of a 45 adapter on it, and every year more and more kids ask me, "What is that symbol?" when I wear it. Some established DJs view spinning CDs as an extension of traditional practices, whereas others treat it as an independent art form.

The right way to go about doing something new would be to start with CD players from the get-go. If you start learning on

CDs now, that's all you know. You get good at that, and it becomes your craft.

—DJ Tron

CD players are about to become much more normal. These new CD mixers are very affordable. I was playing with one the other day, and the effects are incredible. I'm not tempted to go the CD route, but some young whiz kid is going to make a name for himself using that tool creatively.

—DJ DB

I bought a good CD player with double decks about three years ago, and it's taken me three years to get to a point where I can mix with it with my eyes closed. I've replaced everything I could find of my '70s twelve-inch vinyl on CDs. One of my absolute favorite records is Phyllis Hyman's "Loving You Isn't Worth the Pain of Losing You." The beginning is really quiet, and any surface noise is deadly. And all of the sudden I'm hearing it without surface noise, and it's just amazing. That is what hooked me on CDs.

—Peter Calandra

And even though some DJs lament the loss of physical interaction with the playback source that occurs when CDs supplant vinyl, there are arguments in favor of CDs for certain applications, even in the most traditional club set.

I buy new music, but a lot of it is CDs now because I've learned how to use a CD player effectively. Drop mixes are now fearless. When you cue a drop mix on CD, you can cue by frame and do mixes that astound yourself. You don't have to worry about the nuance on your finger. You know when you hit that rubber pad—it's there!

—Peter Calandra

Meanwhile, many DJs are beginning to view the unique sonic properties of CDs as departure points for new musical experiments.

You can't do the same stuff with CDs as with vinyl, but when people started [to DJ] with vinyl, maybe they asked the same questions: "How do we do something nobody else has done before?" When you fast-forward a CD, it sounds fucked up; you can't do that the same way with vinyl. There are ways of creating loops. The destruction of something means the possibility of creating something new, but a lot of DJs are afraid of that.

—Alec Empire

I have tools on my computer so I can slow down or speed up a CD, in real time, with no problem. I actually have more control than on a turntable. So for sampling, CDs are great.

—DJ Lethal

Recordable CDs are really affordable. For the price of one recordable CD, you can have twenty dub plates, which are approximately one hundred dollars a plate, on one CD. That's going to change some things. Probably more in the established club scenario, where the DJ has his equipment—a burnable CD player, stuff like that—right there. Not really in a rave scenario, where the DJ comes in with his box of records for an hour.

—DJ DB

One important thing that I see developing is that the DJ's art is no longer limited only to the format of vinyl. We do a party concept in Berlin called out parties. The idea is not to use vinyl, but only CDs, because we're able to burn our own CDs. You can have more of your own music playing, so the creative musical input is increased. Making dub plates is more expensive [than CDs], and sometimes you think twice.

—Alec Empire

I have a CD burner, which is great. You just make the beats and listen to 'em in your car. You can't bring a turntable in your car.

—DJ Lethal

And CDs aren't the only other playback medium that's gradually being incorporated into more DJ booths.

I was determined to have access to a wider range of sounds than the usual DJ palette, so I have always used CDs, minidiscs, DATs, effects units, computers, and other toys where possible. This is accepted on the trance scene but causes raised eyebrows elsewhere.

Mixmaster Morris

In the trance scene DJs mix on DAT. I use DAT and CDs. The reason the trance scene uses DATs is because of the locations where those psychedelic DJs play. If you're playing on a beach in Goa, [India,] you're not going to use a record. And the majority of people who make that music all circulated it on DATs [among] themselves.

—Paul Oakenfold

Other DJs have been devoting their energies to applying their skills to emerging mediums. Via software like Mixman, cyber-DJs can split a song into its component tracks and reorder them into a whole new remix. Coldcut's V-Jamm software, included on their 1999 *Let Us Replay* CD, takes these ideas even further, allowing users to remix audio and visual materials in real time. Using computers, DJs can program, scratch, and mix whole sets while barely laying a finger on the 1200s.

Coldcut's vision is something that I'm very excited about and watching closely. Right now, they're transcribing the culture of DJs to computer and that's a lot of fun.

—DJ Soul Slinger

Sometimes a phrase meaning becomes outmoded, but the phrase can be recycled—rather than coming up with even more silly acronyms. That's why we talk about a data jockey. It's clear that people are going to want to be entertained on every front. Pumping up the visuals to be as exciting as the audio is, in a decent club, of primary importance. There are various different ways you can link the audio and visual together, from MIDI [muscial instrument digital interface] triggering to using audio-visual samples to color-cycling screen savers. When you integrate all that, you get a very strong synesthetic effect, far greater than what you might expect from just adding the two together. That could be an effective tool for remixing human consciousness, because you're taking control of people's attention via the two most important senses.

—Matt Black (Coldcut)

The idea of using your laptop as your turntable, using two laptops and mixing between them, is pretty exciting. It would be even better if you could do everything all off one laptop, load and mix like that; that's the next big thing. And being able to sync up more elements. Now is just the beginning of real-time manipulation of all sorts of media.

—Jonathan More (Coldcut)

I've been promoting the idea of the data jockey quite stridently, to try [to] keep alive what we've learned so painfully over the years. For me, vinyl is largely a thing of the past, but it took me ages to learn to scratch, and I don't want to give that up. Those skills can be kept alive by grafting them on to new technology. It wasn't that long ago that the phonograph was new technology.

—Matt Black (Coldcut)

The new Coldcut CD or Emergency Broadcast Network's weird video mixing software is one important angle. The future is going to be all about multimedia, downloadable, easy to distribute, and ultra-fragmented. Weird MP3-oriented stuff, although MP3 might not be the format people stick to. But more and more people are going to get into that sense of finding files on line, combining them with weird film or video stuff, making your own mixes or movies.

—DJ Spooky

DJing is a product of technology, as is electronic music, as is all the music we're playing as DJs. As technology moves forward, so do we.

—Richie Hawtin

Thanks to Internet broadcasting, now you don't even need to leave your house or worry about decent radio reception to hear a live DJ set. With computers and ISDN (integrated services digital network) lines, it's completely possible for DJs to be spinning a set in the flesh at one club while a network of wires carries the grooves to other venues all over the world. And with the proliferation of MP3 files, folks can download music from the web without ever visiting a record store.

The Internet is the big vehicle these days. There's the new MP3, which is going to make it easy for people to access CD-quality music on the Internet. I have people from Germany and London and Japan watching my show through the Internet. I get e-mail from people from Brazil. That's uncanny to me still. It makes everything globally accessible. You can't do that with any other format.

—Emily Ng

> That will be the future, getting on line to hear and watch DJs. As long as the Internet and technology doesn't swallow up vinyl, we're okay.
>
> —Andy Smith

> The Internet is a wonderful thing . . . but it's very easy to let technology blind you. I'm very deep into technology myself, but I try to remember that none of this is really worth anything unless you have an actual, physical following. All these Internet-related and web tools are great, but only if there are people [who] really give a damn about what you are about.
>
> —François K.

What are musical equipment manufacturers to do when rebellious youth stop spending their lunch money on distortion pedals and fuzzboxes? Develop more tools that allow DJs access to a wider array of sounds to employ in a set. DJ workstations outfitted with preset sounds, sampling capabilities, and such complement the interface between DJ set and live performance, as explored in the work of Pure Science, Richie Hawtin, Coldcut, and others.

But these machines also have the potential to promote mediocrity. If cheap technology allows a DJ to create a piece of music live that sounds like a new Crystal Method track, why should he or she play the same record as everyone else? Because they're letting their boundaries be set by somebody else: the manufacturer. In the bid to be original, DJs content to rely on preset sounds and rhythms could flood the clubs with a glut of sounds that trigger certain crowd responses, but minus the emotional baggage listeners attach to recognizable songs.

> Samplers and toys sometimes become gimmicks. A lot of DJs don't know what to do with those, because there are perhaps too many options.
>
> —Alec Empire

The interesting trend right now is crossing more equipment with traditional turntables. Manufacturers are coming and giving people these boxes that do everything, these Roland drum machines with sounds and everything [preset]. These things are ten times more powerful than my ten-year old 909, and some of these kids know how to program it and come up with tunes so fast. Seeing equipment like that coming into play, I can imagine a time where we get up there and play with no records at all yet still maintain the essence of the DJ.

—Richie Hawtin (Plastikman)

Some of the equipment they've brought out these days is specifically designed so you can literally write a whole record using the sounds within this keyboard. That degrades the music slightly. When I first started, the drum machines that were around were shit. You didn't have a whole workstation that included every instrument for you. But hopefully this gear will make people appreciate what we do more. It's cool that more people will get into making dance music, but it's adding more negatives than positives, honestly.

—Liam Howlett

There's this new piece of equipment, a rack-mount unit with a little wire that goes into your turntable. No matter what speed you put the decks on, 33 or 45 rpm, the music is going to stay at the same original pitch. Say you've got a bass line and it's too slow—once you put it in your sampler to speed it up, it's going to change pitch. But with this thing, what speed you put the decks on doesn't matter; the original pitch is saved, with no glitches and no sound difference. This is pitch shifting; it's time compression, but keeping the original pitch, which is amazing.

—DJ Lethal

We've invented a device [that] clamps onto your record deck, an extra arm that comes down on to the record and converts the scratching motion into mouse movement, so you use scratching on the turntable to control the computer. We're actually not that far from actually being able to air scratch.

—Matt Black (Coldcut)

The increasing popularity of DJs and dance music also has significant cultural repercussions. Who will be the DJs of the future? What will they opt to play, and what kind of venues will they seek out? Some DJs wring their hands with worry that increasing interest from the mainstream music industry could result in a fiasco similar to the disco bust, whereas others welcome the attention, recognizing that widening the playing field can be a healthy development.

The trend that we've been seeing is a lot more females coming up to us and saying that they've just bought some decks, and they've started to learn to play, and they reckon they'll be ready to roll next year. We'll be seeing a lot more female DJs, and that's a very good thing.

—Kemistry (Kemistry & Storm)

With everything that's available, it's getting almost too easy to move a big club. People doing cutting-edge stuff are going to come up in smaller places and do good stuff there.

—Ben Dubuisson (Purple Penguin)

There are very fruitful potential connections between the art world, the high culture world, and the energy of club culture and techno music.

—Matt Black (Coldcut)

England is a very different place now from 1988 or '92 or '94 or even '96. Club culture has saturated and brainwashed this country to an extent the USA cannot understand. Commercial music rules, like back in the '80s. The majority of independent clubs, labels, distributors, and shops have been forced out of business. People expect to hear the same records everywhere, and they usually do. I find Europe, Japan, [the] USA, and [the] Third World much more interesting places to play because people have fewer preconceptions. In London I find the atmosphere very restrictive as to what I can and cannot play. At every party there's a pack of A&R men and they will be cross all night if you haven't played their latest.

—Mixmaster Morris

Club culture at large has always been incredibly fertile with talent and people that could do amazing things. But most of them haven't really been acknowledged yet. The Grammy Awards just started having a little dance music category two years ago, which is a great step forward. Perhaps the generation that [is] in [its] late teens or early twenties just now [is] finally weaning [itself] off of that guitar-oriented arena rock.

—François K.

I believe that every level of music exists for what it's worth, and each helps the other one. I'm not such a purist. I'm trying to see where everyone's coming from.

—Emily Ng

If going pop means reaching a wider audience, that doesn't bother me. I'll play a hardcore record, but then I'm going to play Ricky Martin's "Livin' la Vida Loca." Just because you don't like that music doesn't mean that Joe Blow in Oshkosh, Wisconsin, isn't going to like it. And I can still get busy and show them what

I can do, and he or she's going to get to see a DJ doing something they've never seen before and relate to them on their level.

—DJ Skribble

When I first got involved, there was no such thing as "This is techno, and this is jungle. . . . " Then everything started splintering off. Everything was divided, and I think that's very negative for the scene. But the music is starting to come back together again a little bit. I'm hearing techno and house in the same room, I'm hearing techno with breakbeats in it, and I'm hearing electro on the dance floor. That's really good, and I hope that trend continues.

—Heather Heart

I'm noticing in certain clubs that the kids don't want to hear house all night long, or hip-hop all night. They want to hear both. Which is the way it was back in the late '80s. And slowly but surely, it's starting to go back that way and become less segregated.

—DJ Skribble

There's a glut of people entering the disc jockey business, and I find it's become a more desperate proposition to get gigs. People seem to be letting go of standards, and that discourages me. Everyone wants to earn a living, but since there are more DJs than there is work, it's gotten a little caustic out there.

—Robbie Leslie

It's almost at a point where if you haven't got a record out, then you're not going to get a booking, unless you've already established your name. DJing is often being used now more as a way to promote records. You've got to spin records.

—Ben Dubuisson (Purple Penguin)

Fatboy Slim isn't doing a live set—he's just DJing to promote [his album].
                                          —Scott Hendy (Purple Penguin)

Cheaper, isn't it? You make more money that way.
                                          —Ben Dubuisson (Purple Penguin)

And regardless of what new skills may enter the DJ's repertory, what untested mediums may emerge to inspire jocks to new flights of invention, one trend seems certain to continue: There will always be a new generation of DJs just around the corner.

I was just watching a little clip of my son scratching on the decks. Before he was two years old, he was scratching with both hands on the fader and the turntable. I can prove it. Our friends are people like Kid Koala and Ollie from the Herbalizer, so he's had a lot of scratch-happy uncles around. And Kid Koala was in the studio a few months ago, and my son went, "I want to scratch...like Eric!" So I give him a scratching lesson every Saturday.
                                          —Matt Black (Coldcut)

My son is the same way. He'll just come downstairs, put on headphones, and put on the records he likes. He doesn't sound that great yet, but he's still a little kid.
                                          —Prince Paul

The future?

Bibliography

Blow, Kurtis, liner notes to *The History of Rap, Vol. 1–3*
    CD anthology, Rhino, 1997

Chaplin, Julia, "Deejays Make the World Go Round,"
    The New York Times, November 8, 1998

Chin, Brian, liner notes to *The Perfect Beats: New York Electro Hip-Hop +
    Underground Dance Classics 1980–1985, Vol. 1–4* CD anthology,
    Tommy Boy/Timber, 1998

Collin, Matthew, with John Godfrey, *Altered State: The Story of Ecstasy Culture
    and Acid House* (London: Serpent's Tail, 1997)

Comer, M. Tye, "Culture Shock: The Rise of the DJ in America,"
    CMJ New Music Monthly, February 1998

Comer, M. Tye, "Paul Oakenfold," *CMJ New Music Monthly*, February 1999

D., Spence, "I'm with the Band," *Raygun*, February 1999

Echlin, Hobey, "Juan Atkins: Craft Worked," *Raygun*, February 1999

Echlin, Hobey, "New Jock City," *Raygun*, February 1999

Fleming, Jonathan, *What Kind of House Party Is This?*
    (Slough, Berkshire, England: MIY Publishing, 1995)

Fukumoto, Bucky, and Jamandru Reynolds, "Turntable Tips from the
    Invisbl Skratch Piklz," *Grand Royal*, issue 4, 1997

BIBLIOGRAPHY

George, Nelson, *Hip Hop America* (New York: Viking, 1998)

Gladstone, Eric, "Prince Paul: The Artist Still Known as Prince,"
   Raygun, February 1999

Goldman, Albert, *Disco* (New York: Hawthorne Books, 1979)

Green, Thomas H., "Back to the Future: Heroes of Electronic Music," *DJ*,
   January 16–29, 1999

Haden-Guest, Anthony, *The Last Party: Studio 54, Disco,
   and the Culture of the Night* (New York: William Morrow and Company,
   1997)

Hager, Steve, *Hip Hop: The Illustrated History of Break Dancing,
   Rap Music and Graffiti* (New York: St. Martin's Press, 1984)

Harvey, Steven, and Patricia Bates, "Behind the Groove,"
   Collusion, September 1983, reprinted in *DJ Times*, March 11–24, 1993

Hershkovits, David, "DJ Spooky: Remixing the Future," *Paper*, November 1998

Howe, Luke, "Jumping Jack Frost" from "Who's Who in Jungle,"
   Generator, September 1995

Joseph, June, "On Wheels of Steel: Beyond Ladies Night with DJ Emily,"
   Paper, May 1998

Kopf, Biba, "Alec Empire: Daft Punk," *The Wire*, December 1997

Ladouceur, Liisa, "Juan Atkins: The Revolution Will Not Be Colorized,"
   Pulse!, November 1998

Martin, Richard, "Prince Paul: The Prince of Amityville,"
   CMJ New Music Monthly, March 1999

Mugridge, Tom, "Do Us a Tape: Juan Atkins," *Muzik*, March 1999

Noble, Peter L., *Future Pop* (New York: Delilah Books, 1983)

Owen, Frank, "Paradise Lost," *Vibe*, November 1993

Poschardt, Ulf, *DJ Culture* (London: Quartet Books, 1998)

Reynolds, Simon, *Generation Ecstasy: Into the World of Techno and Rave Culture* (New York: Little, Brown, 1998)

Rietveld, Hillegonda, "The House Sound of Chicago," in *The Clubcultures Reader,* ed. Steve Redhead with Derek Wynne and Justin O'Connor (Malden, MA: Blackwell Publishers, 1997)

Rose, Tricia, *Black Noise: Rap Music and Black Culture in Contemporary America* (Hanover, NH: University Press of New England, 1994)

Shallcross, Mike, "Juan Atkins: From Detroit to Deep Space," *The Wire,* July 1997

Shapiro, Peter, "Return of the DJ," *The Wire,* June 1997

Shapiro, Peter, "The Primer: Turntablism," *The Wire,* January 1999

Shih, Andy, "DJ Emily," *URB,* March/April 1998

Sicko, Dan, "Richie Hawtin: Reductive Reasoning," *URB,* July/August 1998

Smucker, Tom, "Disco," in *The Rolling Stone Illustrated History of Rock & Roll,* ed. Anthony DeCurtis and James Henke with Holly George-Warren (New York: Random House, 1992)

Wang, Oliver, "Spin Doctors San Francisco Bay Area DJs," *Addicted to Noise,* 1999

Werde, William, "The Real Spin Doctors," *The Washington Post,* February 7, 1999

Whitburn, Joel, *The Billboard Book of Top 40 Hits,* 6th ed. (New York: Billboard Books, 1996)

White, Miles, "The Phonograph Turntable and Performance Practice in Hip Hop Music," *EOL: Peer Reviewed Multimedia Web Journal,* issue 2: "A New Generation of Ethnomusicologists," 1996

Young, Rob, "Plastikman: Immaculate Consumption," *The Wire,* June 1998

Just pop MTV MUSIC GENERATOR into your PlayStation

and prepare to create music magic. Whether you're a beginner

or a whiz, you'll amaze yourself with your homemade jams.

Experiment with 1,500 riffs and 3,000 instrument sounds to create infinite

music possibilities, then make a matching 3-D video

and save it all to a Memory Card to play to your friends. It's MUSIC CREATION

 FOR THE PLAYSTATION... and it rocks. So will you.

EXPRESS YOUR INNER BEATS

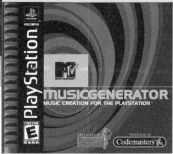

Combine instrument sounds and riffs into cool musical jams, creating rock, hip hop, drum & bass, techno and house tracks.

Produce amazing videos with over 300 shapes, lights and effects, then save your creation to a Memory Card to play for friends.

Create amazing variations by combining blocks of music, then play with up to four friends in jam sessions via Multi Tap.

PUBLISHED BY
Codemasters®

DEVELOPED BY
JESTER INTERACTIVE

www.codemasters.com

 PlayStation ®

6/12